S0-CAE-426

The Bible for Today's World

BOOKS BY DR. CRISWELL . . .

Expository Sermons on Revelation – 5 Vols.

Expository Notes on the Gospel of Matthew

Did Man Just Happen?

Five Great Questions

These Issues We Must Face

The Gospel According to Moses

The Bible for Today's World

The Holy Spirit in Today's World

Our Home in Heaven

The Bible for Today's World

by

W. A. CRISWELL, D.D., Ph.D.
Pastor of the First Baptist Church
Dallas, Texas

ZONDERVAN PUBLISHING HOUSE
GRAND RAPIDS, MICHIGAN

Chapter 10, "The Preservation of the Word of God'" (Second Sermon) appeared in Dr. Criswell's earlier book, *These Issues We Must Face,* and is reprinted by permission.

First printing — 1965
Second printing — 1965
Third printing — 1966

Printed in the United States of America

Dedication

to

DEACON JAMES K. EZELL

and

his devoted wife,

DOROTHY,

whose prayerful interest
and generous philanthropy
make possible the publication
of this volume on

THE ETERNAL WORD OF GOD

Foreword

During the last six months of 1964 I preached nine sermons on the Word of God, the Holy Bible. A faithful deacon in the congregation, James K. Ezell, hearing them felt in his heart that they ought to be published and made available to any and all who would take time to read them.

I preach extemporaneously without notes. I have always preached that way. The messages, therefore, had to be transscribed from tape recordings. This is a most difficult thing to do, especially when names and places and references go beyond the usual acquaintance of ordinary life, and most especially when the preacher repeats too much, explains too much, forgets correct grammar and sentence structure in the heat of his message, and a thousand other things to complicate the transcription. But the work was done through the patient efforts of Mrs. Melvin R. Carter, the typist, and through the grammatical intuition of Mrs. B. B. Binford.

With all my heart, therefore, let me express my gratitude to Deacon James K. Ezell for the gifts that make possible the publication of the book, to Mrs. Melvin R. Carter for the uncounted hours consumed in typing and re-typing the manuscripts, and to Mrs. B. B. Binford for her author's love for making a thing right before it is placed in book form. I have prepared and preached the sermons, I have worked through the manuscripts to see that they carried the message I sought to deliver, but the final production is largely the work of their gracious hands.

Remember as you read them that they are preached sermons, not written lectures. There is a vast difference between. Speaking to a great congregation is an altogether different work from writing out an essay in the sheltered quiet of a library.

There is included in this volume on the Bible an address published by Zondervan in my book, *These Issues We Must*

Face. I have asked Mr. Pat Zondervan if I could include the message here, and he graciously acquiesced. The address is entitled "The Preservation of the Word of God," and forms a companion piece in presenting the same subject from another approach than the sermon by the same title in this series of nine, thus making ten sermons in all.

After finishing her work on the last address, Mrs. Binford wrote: "I trust that this book may bless all who read it and that you may be blessed by having made it available to them." My blessing has richly been bestowed upon me. My faith was strengthened as I prepared and delivered these sermons. Now may God grant that the reader will be blessed as he follows the message I have tried to convey through these pages. The infallible Word of God is our hope for salvation both in this world and in the world that is to come. We share with the devout English poet, William Cowper, his reverence for the Holy Scriptures.

A glory gilds the sacred page,
  Majestic like the sun;
It gives a light to every page;
  It gives but borrows none.

The hand that gave it still supplies
  The gracious light and heat;
His truths upon the nations rise;
  They rise but never set.

Let everlasting thanks be Thine
  For such a bright display
That makes a world of darkness shine
  With beams of heavenly day.

My soul rejoices to pursue
  The steps of Him I love,
Till glory breaks upon my view
  In brighter worlds above.

W. A. CRISWELL

Pastor's Study
First Baptist Church
Dallas, Texas
1965

Contents

1. The Infallible Word of God 13

2. The Foundation for the Faith 27

3. The God-Breathed Word 40

4. Christ and the Prophets 54

5. The Word God Has Spoken 63

6. Jesus and His Bible 75

7. The Words of This Prophecy 87

8. The War Over the Word 98

9. The Preservation of the Word of God . . 109

10. The Preservation of the Word of God . . 120
(*Second Sermon*)

Chapter 1

The Infallible Word of God

> For the prophecy came not in old time by the will of man: but holy men of God spake as they were moved by the Holy Ghost (II Peter 1:21).

From a thoughtful reading of II Peter 1:21 and the preceding verses, 15 through 20, a remarkable fact becomes obvious. It is the paramount place that the Bible, God's Word, "the . . . sure word of prophecy," has in the Apostle's thinking as being "more sure," more reliable in attesting "the power and coming of Jesus Christ" than the personal experiences which the disciples themselves had with the Lord during His earthly ministry.

Simon Peter, the chief Apostle, had said that he knew the time of his own departure was at hand. He had come to that hour when he was soon to "put off this my tabernacle." His decease was not long to be postponed. But to his readers he said in effect, "I shall endeavor to write down these things concerning the deity of our Lord before I am taken from you." He is referring to the gospel of Mark. "For," he says, and I paraphrase, "we have not followed cunningly devised fables. We have not delivered to you myths and legends concerning the heavenly life and miraculous ministry of Jesus our Lord. For we saw those things with our eyes and we heard those things with our ears. Yes," he says, "we even heard the voice of the Father God in heaven saying, 'This is my beloved Son in whom I am well pleased.'" And then he adds this astonishing thing: "But we have a more sure word of prophecy [the Word of God, the Bible]."

This statement is astonishing because he had just said (and again I paraphrase), "I am going to write down these things that I have seen with my eyes and I have heard with my ears, even the voice of the Father in heaven authenticating the ministry of the Divine Son." But now he writes that the surest word of verification for the marvelous, miraculous ministry of the Lord Jesus is not the voice of the Father from heaven. It is not the things the Apostles witnessed having seen them with their own eyes, nor the things they wrote down having heard them with their own ears. But the surest verification for Christ's ministry is the "more sure word of prophecy." That is almost unbelievable but that is what Peter writes.

Then he describes that sure word of prophecy. "For [the sure word of] prophecy came not in old time by the will of man." Man did not think it up, nor was it human genius that wrote it down. It was not Shakespearian or Miltonian or Homeric genius or inspiration. But holy men of God spoke as they were moved by the Holy Ghost. Now that is the Biblical idea of the inspired Word of God. Holy men of God wrote it down, they spoke, used words and syllables, sentences and paragraphs, language, ideas and thoughts. They wrote as they were moved by the Holy Spirit of God.

MODERN IDEAS CONCERNING THE ACCURACY OF SCRIPTURE

How different is the modern, popularly accepted idea of the writing of the Holy Scriptures! I shall quote from an eminent theologian who is apologizing for the Bible, and in quoting his testimony, I am giving you the attitude of almost the entire modern theological world. He is not unique in his views; he is just expressing the persuasion of the majority of contemporary theologians. As he apologizes for the Bible, he says: "Of course, there are scientific errors in the Bible. However, we can excuse such mistakes on the grounds that the Bible is not a textbook of science and therefore we do not expect it to be scientifically accurate."

I agree with the theologian on one thing, that the Bible

is not a textbook on science. The Bible is the Word of God written for the salvation of our souls that we might be delivered from damnation and hell. If a man ever sees the face of God, if a man ever goes to heaven, he must go by the revelation and truth imparted to us in the holy Word of God. There is no other way to be saved. "There is none other name under heaven given among men whereby we must be saved." There is only one way to be saved and that way is revealed in the sacred Book. We are not to read the Bible as a textbook on civics, geometry, astronomy, cosmogony or anthropology. It is a book of God to show us how to be saved. I agree, therefore, that it is not a textbook on science.

The rest of the statement is blasphemy: "Of course, there are scientific errors in the Bible. However, we can excuse such mistakes . . . we do not expect it to be scientifically accurate." My brother, if the Bible is not also scientifically accurate it is not, to me at least, the Word of God. I have a very plain reason for that. The Lord God who made this world and all the scientific marvels which we are now discovering in it—that same Lord God knew all these things from the beginning. We do not surprise Him with our discovery of the waves on which our church services are broadcast and televised. God made those waves in the beginning and we have just discovered them. Jet propulsion that speeds planes along through the sky is not a surprise to God. He made that force in the beginning. Now if the Bible is the Word of God, and if God inspired it, then it cannot contain any scientific mistakes because God knew every truth and fact of science from the beginning.

When we compare the Word of God with science, much of which is actually hypothetical, theoretical guess-work by men who are mostly darkened in counsel; when we come to compare the Bible with these modern pseudo-scientific theories and postulates and hypotheses, let us be careful of two things. First, let us be very certain that we are conversant with the Word of God. Let us be sure that we know the Word of God when we start thinking about the scientific facts that apparently contradict the Bible.

Some time ago there was a world-famous minister who was also a scientist, who loved both God and His marvelous works. From one side of this nation to the other, he published in all the newspapers an advertisement saying that he would give $1,000 to anyone, anywhere, anytime who could point out to him one scientific error in the Bible. He received a letter, among others, from a graduate of the University of Michigan who resided in Detroit. She was claiming the $1,000 for, she declared, she had found a certain scientific error in the Bible. It is said to be true, she pointed out, that the Garden of Eden was in the Valley of Mesopotamia. (That is correct because the Euphrates River ran through it.) But she added, "It has been scientifically demonstrated that no apples can grow in the Mesopotamian Valley, and we are told in the Bible that Adam and Eve were driven out of the Garden of Eden because they ate of the fruit of an apple tree. Therefore," she said, "I am waiting for my $1,000."

The minister wrote back to her: "My dear, the Bible mentions the fruit of the tree of the knowledge of good and evil; it does not mention an apple." The woman finally wrote back, after thorough investigation, and said: "I cannot find in the Bible where it says *apple,* but I know it is there because my teacher told me so."

Let me tell you something I found this week. Reading in preparation for this sermon, I stumbled across the debate concerning the adoption of the Gregorian calendar. That is the calendar that we live by now. It is the calendar that has been adopted by all of the civilized world. As you know, January first begins our New Year in the Gregorian calendar. Did you know that when the Gregorian calendar was adopted and men were discussing it and debating it, its beginning date, January first, was bitterly opposed on the ground that Eve ate an apple and apples do not ripen until September? Therefore, they argued, the year began in the

Bible in September—all on the basis of Eve's eating an apple in the fall of the year!

I am just saying that first, we must be sure and certain that we are conversant with the Word of God and what it says.

Second, let us be sure of our scientific facts. True science is always changing. It is like a chicken, always moulting. Did you know that it has been estimated that in the library of the Louvre in Paris, France, there are at least three and one-half miles of books on science, which books are obsolete, outdated, outmoded, so that nobody ever reads a syllable of them anymore? A book of science ten years old is nine years obsolete. Just think of that!

Now, what if you were to take this Bible and update it to the latest scientific fads and theories and hypotheses? Think of what you would do to the Bible. Think of what you would have done to the Bible in 1000 B.C. had you updated it then to the latest scientific fad. What would you have done to the Bible in 500 B.C.? What would you have done in A.D. 1? What would you have done in A.D. 500? What would you have done in A.D. 1000? What would have become of the Bible had you put into it all of the scientific ideas and conjurations and monstrosities of A.D. 1660? You would have had to have a new edition in 1760 and another one in 1860. And had we done so in 1960 we should be looking for a new edition in 1970. Had you updated the Bible according to the latest scientific fads in any generation, in fact, it would have been filled with pseudo-scientific absurdities and nonentities.

Did you know that in 1861 (that is just about 100 years ago) the French Academy of Science published a little brochure in which they stated fifty-one scientific facts that controverted the Word of God? Today there is not a scientist in the world who believes a single one of those fifty-one so-called scientific facts that in 1861 were published as controverting the Word of God. Not a one!

THE SCIENTIFIC BACKGROUND OF THE WRITERS OF THE BIBLE

The most phenomenal thing of all this is that the Bible, this Word of God, has not changed. Every syllable of it is just as it was when God, through the Holy Spirit, wrote it down. The Bible was written by forty authors over a period of one thousand and five hundred years. They did not know each other. There was no collaboration, no collusion. And they wrote, each one of them, as they were inspired of the Holy Spirit of God, over a period of one thousand and five hundred years. Yet with all of the unbelievable, weird, wild background of the days in which they lived there is no repercussion of any of that darkness and superstition in the Word of God.

For instance, in Acts 7:22, we are told that Moses was learned in all of the science of the Egyptians. Moses was learned in all of the wisdom—all the *sophia*—of the Egyptians. He knew all the latest scientific fads, he was abreast with all of the latest scientific discoveries in his day.

Now we can know exactly what Moses was taught. Archaeologists have dug up and put together all of these things that Moses read, all the textbooks of science in his day. They are now before us and we can study them just as Moses did in his day. Those Egyptians were brilliant people. They had a science of cosmogony, the origination of the world, the creation of the world. Those Egyptian scientists believed in Moses' day that this earth was hatched out of a great cosmic egg, an egg that had wings and was flying around through space. According to the latest Egyptian scientific facts, as this enormous winged egg flew around, the processes of mitosis on the inside of the shell were completed and out hatched this world. Out of that flying ovum, here we are! That was the latest scientific theory among those who taught in the days of Moses.

So I turn over here to the Word of God expecting to read about that flying egg, for after all, Moses was learned in all the science of the Egyptians. But I find nothing at all about that enormous hatchery. Instead of that, I read of creation in the sublimest words that man could pen: "In the beginning God created the heavens and the earth."

Those Egyptians also had a science of astronomy. They believed that the sun was the reflection of the light on the earth, and that the earth was the center of this universe. But in Genesis I find that Moses reversed the order—it is the sun that gives light to the earth.

The Egyptians had a science of anthropology. They were naive evolutionists. They believed that mankind sprang from little white worms that they found in the slime and ooze and mud of the alluvial deposit after the Nile's annual overflow. Perhaps they supposed so because they had observed the metamorphosis of a caterpillar into a butterfly. The scientists of Moses' day with their theory of evolution from worms were not far behind those today who would have you believe that your remote ancestors were fleabitten apes hanging by their tails in a primeval jungle. I read in the Bible that Moses was learned in all the science of the Egyptians. But he says nothing about those little white worms and how we were descended from them. Instead he writes in the most majestic language in human speech: "And God said, Let us make man in our image, after our likeness. . . . So God created man in His own image, in the image of God created He him; male and female created He them."

The Bible is thus throughout the whole Word of God. It does not reflect the scientific background of the day in which it was written. The Bible is a historical book but it has been kept from error by the Holy Spirit of God.

In the background of many of the centuries of the Bible is the Chaldean civilization. They also had definite scientific hypotheses concerning the origin of the world and all things therein. Their cosmogony went like this: the earth is one gigantic monster, covered with feathers and scales. The feathers and the scales are the rocks and the trees. As a flea lives in the hair on the hide of a dog, so the human race lives on the hide of this big monster and we burrow into the rocks and live beneath the trees. Then, they said, if you dig down too far and hurt that monster, he will shake himself and buildings will fall down. They had a scientific proof for their theory. For they did dig down into the earth (for such things as gold and silver), and earthquakes did happen and buildings did fall down. Such was their scientific proof for their theory of what kind of a world we live in. But in all of the Word of God you will not find a semblance of that monstrous weirdness.

Consider the Babylonian people. Much of the Bible is written against the cultural and scientific background of their civilization. The Babylonians also had a theory of anthropology, of human creation. They said that in the beginning there was a monster by the name of Tia-mat and a great god by the name of Marduk. These two had a fierce battle and Marduk overcame Tia-mat. When Marduk flattened out Tia-mat, his body became the earth. Then, according to the latest Babylonian science of those days, Marduk spit and where he spat men came up, much like the dragonseed that Jason sowed. And then the men spat, and wherever the men spat women came up. And then the women spat, and wherever the women spat animals came up. That was the latest scientific theory in Babylonian days. Do you find any of that idiocy in the Word of God? Yet all of such mythology and a thousand other things just as wild and weird and unimaginable were currently believed in the days when the Bible was written. Such was the science of that day.

THE LATEST SCIENCE IN THE HOLY SCRIPTURES

Let us turn now to the Word of God to see what kind of scientific background is written here large upon the pages of God's holy Book. Choosing from a multitude of passages, let us turn first to Job 26:7: "God stretcheth out the north over the empty place, and hangeth the earth upon nothing."

Look at that north star up there in the universe of God shining alone! "And God hangeth the earth upon nothing." Did you know that human beings for thousands of generations before and after Job wrote these scientific words believed that the earth was sustained by some kind of solid foundation? Every one did. Every civilization did. Every culture did. Every nation did.

The Egyptians said that the world is sustained by five great pillars, one at each corner and one in the middle. Five great pillars, they said, sustained the earth. When Job wrote, "God hangeth the world upon nothing," that was the science of the Egyptians. The Greeks were taught to believe that this world is held up by an immense giant by the name of Atlas, upon whose great shoulders and back the world rested. That is what the learned, sophisticated Greeks believed. The Hindu scientist and theologian believed that this earth is sustained on the back of a gigantic elephant, that thc elephant stands on the back of an enormous sea-turtle, and that the sea-turtle swims in a cosmic ocean. Then he ran out of imagination and quit without saying what the ocean stands on. But that was their latest scientific theory in the day when Job wrote, "God hangeth the earth on nothing."

Turn now to Isaiah 11:12: "And he [God] shall set up an ensign for the nations, and shall assemble the outcasts of Israel, and gather together the dispersed of Judah from the four corners of the earth." All the infidels and cynics and critics and new lights in theology say, "See, look what Isaiah wrote: 'God shall gather the dispersed of Judah from the four corners of the earth.' Therefore, in keeping with the scientific theories of his day, Isaiah believed the earth was flat and that it had four corners." This is one of the passages they quote to criticize.

Remembering that Isaiah wrote not in English but in Hebrew, and that to know what Isaiah said one must read the original Hebrew text, I looked it up. His Hebrew idiom is altogether different from our English idiom but both mean the same thing. We say "the four corners of the earth" meaning the whole world. For example, during a violent storm at sea when the passengers on the boat became afraid, the captain called them all together and said: "Now you listen to me. I have sailed this boat to the four corners of the seas and I tell you this wind is not dangerous. This is just a hard blow." Another example comes from signs the United States government placed in all the post offices, reading, "Join the United States Marines and visit the four corners of the earth."

Isaiah presents the same meaning in Hebrew. The Hebrew idiom meaning "to the farthest extremity" is taken from the spreading of a bird's wings. The Hebrew word for the two wings of a bird is *kenepoth.* Isaiah says in Hebrew idiom, "And he shall gather together the dispersed of Judah from the four *kenepoth* of the earth — from the four *wings* of the earth." Thus I discovered why the Hebrew used the idiom *winged* to refer to the uttermost parts of the earth. It was their word for "extremity." When a bird spread out its wings, there was an extremity accurately described. That is as far as the extremity would stretch. The prophet could have said, "from the four parts of the compass — north, south, east and west — God is going to gather His children together." But he more graphically said it the other way.

Now it is just such discrepancies in translations that seem baffling. But if you know your Bible you will not be confused by the critics. These so-called scientific errors in the Bible melt away under close analysis.

Turn to Isaiah 40:22. "It is he that sitteth upon the circle of the earth." When Isaiah wrote that, there was not a living man in the world who believed that the world was round. Not one. Isaiah lived around 750 B.C. and there was not a man in the earth before him nor after him for countless generations, who believed that the earth was round. But look what Isaiah wrote by the Spirit of God: "He that sitteth upon the circle of the earth."

Let us turn again to I Corinthians 15:39: "All flesh is not the same flesh: but there is one kind of flesh of men, another flesh of beasts, another of fishes, and another of birds." We could translate the passage like this: "All protoplasm is not the same protoplasm. There is one protoplasm of men, there is another protoplasm of beasts, there is another protoplasm of fishes, there is another protoplasm of birds." That is what Paul wrote.

But when men discovered cells, and when on the inside of cells they discovered protoplasm, it became the scientific rage to avow that all life was made out of the same and identical stuff—protoplasm. But Paul wrote that that was not so. He wrote that there is a protoplasm of men and that the protoplasm of men is not like the protoplasm of animals; and the protoplasm of animals is not like the protoplasm of fishes; and the protoplasm of fishes is not like the protoplasm of birds. After we became more learned and our scientists finally discovered the truth, we found it to be exactly as Paul wrote. The cytoplasm and the nuclei on the inside of the cells of a man are altogether different from the cytoplasm and the nuclei on the inside of the cells of any other animal or beast or bird, and all of them are different from one another. Isn't that remarkable?

THE ETERNAL GOD AND THE ETERNAL WORD

Turn to Hebrews 1:10-12, which quotes from Psalm 102: 25-27: "Thou, Lord, in the beginning hast laid the foundation of the earth; and the heavens are the works of thine hands: They shall perish; but thou remainest; and they all shall wax old as doth a garment; And as a vesture shalt thou fold them up, and they shall be changed: but thou art the same, and thy years shall not fail."

Did you know that here is a better scientific statement of Sir James Jeans' book, *The Wider Aspects of Cosmology* than Jeans himself wrote? For he finally came to the conclusion that this universe is like a great clock that is running down, running down. Every time there is liberation of energy, the complex molecular structure of a substance dissolves, breaks down into simpler construction. But you can never put that energy back into it again and you can never build it up again. This whole universe is like a vast wound-up clock. It is running down, running down, running down, and finally someday even the sun will go out and this universe will be extinct.

"Thou, Lord, [made the heavens and the earth] in the beginning [God wound it up] . . . They shall perish; but thou remainest; and they all shall wax old as doth a garment; And as a vesture shalt thou fold them up, and they shall be changed [they shall die]: but thou art the same, and thy years shall not fail."

The latest scientific theories are confirmed by the Word of God. To take just one other example, turn to Hebrews 11:3: "Through faith we understand that the worlds were framed by the word of God, so that things which are seen were not made of the things which do appear." Let me paraphrase that: "So that the things that are visible are made out of entities that are invisible." Did you ever hear a finer statement of the molecular, atomic, nature of this universe in substance and reality than that? "The things that are visible, the things that we see, are made out of things, entities, that are invisible, made out of things you cannot see."

From beginning to ending there is not a word or a syllable or a revelation in the Word of God that has contradicted or ever will contradict any true, substantiated scientific fact. The reason is very simple. The Lord God who inspired the Book is the Lord God who made these things from the beginning. That is why when the Lord speaks through His servants, you can base your life and your soul and your salvation on what God has said.

There is not a more familiar story in the annals of literature than the story that describes the death of the immortal Scot poet and novelist, Sir Walter Scott. As he lay dying he turned to his son-in-law, Lockhart, and said to him, "Son, bring me the Book." There was a vast library in Walter Scott's home and, bewildered, the son-in-law said, "Sir, what book? Which book?" The dying bard replied, "My son, there is just one Book. Bring me *the* Book." It was then that Lockhart went to the library and brought to Sir Walter Scott the Bible.

"There's just one Book," cried the dying sage,
"Read me the old, old story."
And the winged words that can never age
Wafted him home to Glory.
There's just one Book.

There's just one Book for the tender years,
One Book alone for guiding
The little feet through the joys and fears,
The unknown days are hiding.
There's just one Book.

There's just one Book for the bridal hour,
One Book of love's own coining;
Its truths alone lend beauty and power,
To vows that lives are joining.
There's just one Book.

There's just one Book for life's gladness,
One Book for the toilsome days,
One Book that can cure life's madness,
One Book that can voice life's praise.
There's just one Book.

There's just one Book for the dying,
One Book for the starting tears,
And one for the soul that is going home,
For the measureless years.
There's just one Book.

— ANONYMOUS

"For the prophecy came not . . . by the will of man: but holy men of God spake as they were moved by the Holy Ghost" (II Peter 1:21). And this is the inerrant, infallible, holy, eternal Word of the living God. "The grass withereth, the flower fadeth; but the Word of our God shall stand for ever" (Isaiah 40:8). "Heaven and earth will pass away, but my word will not pass away" (Mark 13:31). "For ever, O Lord, thy word is firmly fixed in the heavens" (Psalm 119:89, RSV). Oh, what a blessedness, what a holiness, what a foundation, eternal and immovable, is the living Word of the living God! "And his name is called The Word of God" (Revelation 19:13).

Chapter 2

The Foundation for the Faith

> But the word of the Lord endureth for ever. And this is the word which by the gospel is preached unto you (I Peter 1:25).

This series of sermons concerns the enduring, unchanging, eternal Word of God. I Peter 1:23, 24 reads: "Being born again, not of corruptible seed, but of incorruptible, by the word of God, which liveth and abideth for ever. For all flesh is as grass and all the glory of man as the flower of the grass." Then the Apostle Simon Peter quotes Isaiah 40:8: "The grass withereth, the flower fadeth: but the word of our God shall stand for ever." Next, he adds by inspiration, "And this is the word which by the gospel is preached unto you." It is the Gospel wherein we are born again by the Word of God. So I speak of the foundation for the faith, which foundation is the abiding, enduring, incorruptible and eternal Word of God.

One day an infidel challenged a brilliant minister to a debate on the inspiration of the Bible. When the time came, the atheist stood up first to deny the Word of God. He opened his remarks with these words: "Now in this debate we shall not turn for proof to the Bible, itself, for you cannot prove a thing by the thing itself. You cannot test a thing by the thing itself. Thus we are not to prove the Bible by the Bible, itself. Rather, our debate is to concern extraneous matters and materials." It was a very unusual premise.

After he sat down, the minister stood up and said: "All of us have listened to the ground rules laid down by my opponent, this atheist, that in this debate we are not to appeal to the Bible, itself; for he says that we cannot prove a thing by the thing itself or test a thing by the thing itself, but that we must turn to extraneous evidences." Then said this brilliant minister: "That would be as though a man who had a ranch went to the assayer and said, 'You know, I have found an outcropping of quartz on my ranch and in it are some yellow particles. I think that I have gold in those mountains.' The assayer would reply, 'Well, bring me a piece of that quartz with those gold specks in it,' and the ranchman would say, 'Oh, no, indeed not. For you cannot prove a thing by the thing itself nor can you test a thing by the thing itself. You take one of the bricks out of the walls of your house, and you test it, and tell me whether or not there is gold on my ranch.' "

Then the minister said, "Or it would be as though a man feared someone was poisoning him by putting potassium cyanide in his sugar. So he went to the chemist and said: 'I am fearful that someone is seeking to poison me. I am afraid there is cyanide in my sugarbowl.' So the chemist said, 'Well, you bring me your bowl of sugar and we will test it.' 'Oh, no,' said the man, 'you cannot prove a thing by the thing itself, nor can you test a thing by the thing itself. You go to the kitchen and get your salt shaker off of the table and test it, and tell me whether there is cyanide in my sugarbowl or not.' " Then the minister went right ahead, as he should have done, and looked at the Bible, itself, to see whether or not it is God-breathed (the actual meaning of the word "inspired"). Now, that is what we are going to do in this sermon.

THREE FOUNDATIONAL OBSERVATIONS CONCERNING THE BIBLE

Three things I have chosen to discuss that are to be found in the Bible, the foundation of our faith—three very patent things evident on every sacred page.

First: All that we know of God and all that we know of

true religion are to be found between the covers of this sacred volume. You could make a life study of the natural world and you could philosophize about it endlessly. The heathen did; the pagan did. In this approach you would learn about as much concerning the Creator of this world as you would about the architect of a palace by gazing upon it. You would come to the conclusion that the world was created by someone of vast, illimitable resources—but that is all. Further, you might look at a beautiful sunset or a glorious rainbow and surmise that whoever created them must have loved things beautiful—but that is all. Again, you might listen to the roar of thunder and watch the flash of lightning and surmise that whoever is their primal cause is one of vast power—but that is all. You might look within yourself and philosophize about your knowledge of right from wrong and conclude that whoever created you is a Lord of righteousness. But you could never know who that Creator is, you could never know His name, you could never know His character and His personality, were He not self-revealed, were He not self-disclosed, as He is in this holy Book. All that we know of a personal God is revealed in His Word, the Bible.

All that you know of Jesus is revealed in these sacred pages. The few exceptions are the sentences in secular history by Tacitus and by Suetonius, Roman historians who were writing after the death of Caesar Nero, and in Pliny's letters. In describing the life of Nero, Tacitus said the Emperor laid upon the followers of Christ the blame for the burning of Rome. Therefore the historian had to explain to a world that had never heard of Christ just who Christ was: a Jew who was crucified under the Roman Procurator, Pontius Pilate. This is the one sentence in Tacitus. Likewise, there is one sentence in Suetonius describing Christians. That is all, aside from a sentence in one of Pliny's letters and a spurious paragraph in Josephus. Therefore if we are to know anything about the Lord Jesus Christ, if we are introduced to Him, we must come to that knowledge through the pages of the Bible.

During seminary days, I was very much impressed by the remark of my Greek teacher, one of the far-famed scholars of all time. When we had finished the course of the New Testament, he said: "Young gentlemen, you have studied Christ Himself, the whole Christ, all of Christ. When you study the Bible, when you study the gospels, you are studying the Lord, Himself. For all we know of the Lord is encompassed in these sacred pages."

All that we know of salvation we read in the Book. "What must I do to be saved?" you ask. Let a heathen philosopher reply; let a pagan theorist reply; let a metaphysician reply; let a Hindu religionist reply; let a pseudo-scientist reply. Listening to them, you are as lost and as darkened in counsel as you would be if you had never asked the question. There is no light of salvation in them.

All we know of the future is revealed in this sacred Book. Seers in ancient times have peered through the long vistas of the centuries and have been baffled in words and in wisdom as they tried to ferret out some answer to the question of what lies ahead. But there is no revelation other than that to be found in the immutable Word of the immutable God. Men do not, cannot know the future. But God knows it and reveals it, and this revelation becomes one of the mighty reasons for the inspiration of the Scriptures.

This eternal truth gives rise to the increasingly violent and vicious attacks upon the inspiration of the Holy Scriptures. "If the foundations be destroyed," cried the Psalmist in Psalm 11:3, "what can the righteous do?" If the Bible is described and accepted as being the work of the natural, ordinary human mind, then the foundation of our faith, the revelation of God, our hope of salvation, any knowledge we have of the Lord or of the future is thereby swept away in the so-called myth and legend and fantasy out of which somebody is supposed to have spun these holy words. But this is not true. God is in this Holy Book and all that we know of God and of true religion is revealed in the pages of the Bible.

THE BIBLE'S UNITY IN DIVERSITY

I have a second observation as I hold the Word of God in my hand. Its one theme produces an amazing and astonishing unity in diversity. I carefully worked out that sentence. Let me repeat it. Its one great theme reveals an astonishing and amazing unity in diversity. There is one thread, a golden thread—I like to call it a scarlet thread—there is one golden, scarlet thread through all the Word of God. There is one tremendous theme in all the Word of God. It is proclaimed in the ancient day like this, "There is Someone who is coming." It is announced in the day of His incarnation like this, "Someone is come." Finally it is prophesied in the day of the apocalyptic consummation like this, "Someone is coming again." This one great theme binds the whole Book together. There is a Saviour who is coming. There is a Saviour who has come. There is a Lord Omnipotent who is coming again. And that one vast theme has produced an astonishing and amazing unity in the diversity of its unfolding in the pages of the Holy Scriptures.

There are at least forty writers in the Bible. They lived over a period of more than fifteen hundred years. They did not know each other. They were separated by culture and background, by civilization, by every kind and type of life. And yet for more than fifteen hundred years, over forty writers were speaking the same things, introducing the same revelation, repeating the same incomparable Word.

In the Holy Book you will find romance, as in the story of Sarah or Rebekah or Rachel or Ruth. You will find law, the incomparable precepts of the Mosaic legislature. You will find history, the story of the kings of Israel, of Judah and of the kingdoms of the world. You will find poetry, as in the incomparably beautiful twenty-third Psalm. You will find proverbs. You will find prophecy. One-third of the Bible is prophecy. And yet through the gamut of its many-faceted literatures there is one great, holding, constant theme: The Lord is at hand. "Maranatha! Maranatha! the Lord is coming!"

You cannot divide this Book. You cannot separate it. It is one: the old covenant, the new covenant, the Old Testament, the New Testament. What is enfolded in the Old Testament is unfolded in the New. What lies latent in the Old Testament is patent in the New. What is promised and prophesied in the Old is produced and revealed in the New. They are one. "God, who at sundry times and in divers manners spake unto the fathers by the prophets, has in these last days spoken unto us by his Son [the Word of God]" (Hebrews 1:1, 2). Whether the words are spoken by the prophets beholding the future, or whether they are spoken by the voice of the apostles declaring their fulfillment, they are all one—the Word of God. The Old and the New Covenants cannot be separated.

In my preparation for this sermon, I read of a young fellow who lived in a large city which is built upon tall hills. This young fellow had an old jalopy, a car of ancient vintage. In order to get up one of those high hills, he needed a running start so that he could make it up to the top. He got himself ready, and got his contraption all geared up, but when he came to the intersection before the hill, he discovered that to his right was an automobile coming, followed by another. He had barely time to figure it all out in that split moment. By letting the first car go by and then by gunning his pile of junk before the second car came to the intersection, he had just time to go between the two automobiles and scramble up the hill. The only miscalculation was that he had not noticed that the front car was towing the second car. They were tied together with a steel cable. When the young fellow got out of the hospital and got through paying the bill, he had learned this great theological lesson, that it is very difficult to divide things that are bound together!

It is just so in the Word of God. This piece belongs to this piece; this section is inextricably connected with this section; and the whole thing is welded together by the hand of the Lord. That is the second observation concerning the Holy Book, its marvelous unity in diversity. It has one supreme announcement and one incomparably glorious message.

THE ONLY BOOK IN THE WORLD WRITTEN BY TRUE PROPHETS

Now, notice a third thing as you hold the Book in your hand. It is a book of prophecy, of revelation. The Book's marvelous announcements gave rise to a miraculous phenomenon which you will find alone and only in the Bible; namely, the prophets and the spirit of prophecy and the prophecies that they made. In no other religion, in no other culture, in no other philosophy, in no other part of human life or experience will you find that phenomenon. There is only one religion in the world, there is only one place in the world where you will find a prophet and prophecy, and that is in the Word of God. The reason is very plain. There is no one who knows the future and there is no one who can foretell it except the Lord God. He alone controls and guides the future and by His sovereign grace brings things that He has said to an open and final consummation.

"The secret things belong unto the Lord our God," said Moses in Deuteronomy 29:29. It is only "those things which are revealed [that] belong unto us and to our children for ever." The secret things, the things that lie ahead belong unto the Lord our God. He alone knows them and can reveal them.

I hold the Book in my hand and I read predictions of events made thousands and thousands of years ahead. I read predictions centuries and centuries ahead. Sometimes these prophecies concern vast movements on the stage of human history. Sometimes they concern tiny inconsequentials that God saw in the mosaic of the world that was yet to come. But whether great or large they are a sign of the presence of the True God.

One of the interesting things that you will find in the Book is how the Lord God challenges the gods of the nations and the gods of the heathen. Listen to Him as He speaks to them in Isaiah 41:23: "Shew the things that are to come hereafter, that we may know that ye are gods." You so-called gods of Persia, of Assyria, of Egypt, of the Orient, of the Occident — wherever there is one who thinks himself wise or as a god—stand up and show the things that are to come hereafter that we may know that you are gods. "I am the Lord . . . behold . . . new things do I declare: before they spring forth I tell you of them" (Isaiah 42:8, 9).

I turn the page to Isaiah 45:1: "Thus saith the Lord to his anointed to Cyrus . . . ." What an amazing thing! This prophet Isaiah is speaking in 750 B.C., and Cyrus never came on the scene of history until 550 B.C. Two hundred years before Cyrus came on the pages of history, the Lord God called his name. The Lord called his name two hundred years before Cyrus came to be the leader of the Medo-Persian armies.

There is a difference between prophecy and surmise. Suppose we have a Gallup Poll to make a survey of all our United States and it is revealed that in a coming election Thomas B. Dewey is going to be elected President of the United States. So the New York *Herald Tribune,* on the basis of one of those supposedly infallible surveys, publishes in big black headlines, *Dewey Elected President.* That is your fine poll survey! But who is elected? Harry Truman! Isn't that accurate prognostication!

To show the difference between man's surmising and prophecy is very simple to do. When a poll is taken, or when a politician in Washington surveys the nation and predicts that this coming November so-and-so is going to be elected, that is political sagacity, not prophecy. But suppose the same politician were to stand up in Washington and name the man that is going to be elected in A.D. 2164.

That would be prophecy. To stand up and call the name of the President of the United States two hundred years hence is prophecy.

In the forty-fifth chapter of Isaiah, God foretells the coming of Cyrus two hundred years before he came into history. That is prophecy as it can only be known by God, the Holy One of Israel, the One who could say to Cyrus before he was even born, "I have even called thee by name: I have surnamed thee, though thou hast not known me. I am the Lord, and there is none else, there is no God beside me." For God sees the whole consummation of the age, declaring the end from the beginning, and from ancient times the things that are not yet done. Only God can thus prophesy and that is what He has done in His Word, the Bible. Man may surmise as to the future; but God alone ("I am God and there is none like me") can prophesy.

There is a story that when Cyrus came into Babylon and took over the rule of the civilized world, there was one Zerubbabel who came to Cyrus and showed him in the Word of God how the Lord had called his name two hundred years before he appeared at the gates of the Chaldean Empire. When Cyrus read it he was amazed and thereupon made the decree that is recorded in the first chapter of Ezra, giving Israel an opportunity to go back home to build their kingdom and their city, Jerusalem, with its sacred Temple.

One of the most eloquent passages in Josephus is his description of the onward march of Alexander the Great after he had swept through Asia Minor, as he came down the seacoast in order to conquer Egypt. When he came by little Palestine, he turned aside and went north to Jerusalem. Josephus says that when Alexander the Great appeared at the gates of Jerusalem, the high priest in all of his glorious robes came out with his fellow priests to meet the Emperor. After Alexander had worshiped God, the high priest showed him from the prophet Daniel the prediction of his coming and the great success by which God would crown his pas-

sage. As a result, Alexander spared the Temple and Jerusalem and all Judah. What an amazing thing! This is of God.

Many times will you find the conflict between the false unbeliever and the true Word of God in the Holy Scriptures. Jeremiah at one time was carrying around on his neck an iron yoke (Jeremiah 27, 28). He was parabolizing to the city of Jerusalem, preaching by example a sermon that God was going to desert and destroy that place, and that the people were going to be sold into captivity because of their iniquity. A prophet by the name of Hananiah met Jeremiah in front of the priests and the people and broke off that iron yoke from Jeremiah's neck, saying in effect, "We are not going into Babylonian captivity." Jeremiah stood up after the yoke was broken off his neck to say that "this nation and this king and these princes shall surely go into captivity and this shall be the sign: Hananiah, thou false prophet, thou shalt die this year" (see Jeremiah 28:14-17). Two months later Hananiah died. And before long the people were carried away into Babylonian captivity.

A similar story is told in I Kings 22 of the prophet Micaiah. Ahab, king of Israel, called Jehoshaphat, king of Judah, and said, "Let's go up to Ramoth-gilead and take it; it belongs to us." But Jehoshaphat, who was a godly man, wanted the Lord's confirmation. After all the prophets had told them to go to battle, Jehoshaphat said, "All these paid prophets say 'Go up.' Isn't there one other prophet here?"

Ahab answered, "Yes, his name is Micaiah, but I hate him, I hate him, I hate him."

Jehoshaphat said, "Don't say that. Bring him before me."

So they called Micaiah and they said, "Micaiah, all of these prophets say to go up and take Ramoth-gilead for the Lord is giving it to us."

Micaiah's reply was, "By the help of God, I shall say what God says, I shall deliver the Word of the Lord." And when Micaiah spoke, he foretold the death of Ahab and the destruction of the armies of Israel.

Then Zedekiah, the leader of the false prophets, went

over and smote Micaiah on his cheek and said, "Which way went the Spirit of the Lord from me to speak to you?"

Micaiah replied, "In the day when you crawl into your chambers in shame and disgrace, you will learn." Then he turned to Ahab and said, "If you return alive from this battle this day, God has not spoken to me."

You remember the rest of the story. Ahab disguised himself so that no one would know him and went out into the war against Ramoth-gilead. And the Book says that an archer drew back a bow at random, and let an arrow fly without even aiming; and that arrow found a joint in the harness of Ahab and pierced his heart and his blood flowed out in the chariot. They brought him home and washed the chariot at the well of Jezreel in the region where Naboth's body had been slain by Jezebel and Ahab; and the dogs licked up the blood of Ahab as they washed the chariot. Then the story ends with these awesome words, ". . . according to the Word of the Lord" (I Kings 22:38).

One might speak of how the prophets described in minutiae the destruction of Tyre and how it came to pass; of how Nahum described the destruction of Nineveh, and of how Diodorus Siculus, the Greek historian, inadvertently described the destruction of great Nineveh exactly according to the prophecy of Nahum; or of what Jeremiah said about the destruction of Jerusalem.

OUR PRESENT TIMES IN THE LIGHT OF PROPHECY

Let us look at the present times in the light of prophecy. Prophecy does not just concern former times. The Lord speaks to us of today. He reveals to us the things of this present age. An example of prophecy that reaches to us today is found in Daniel 2, in the vision of the great image. In the course of the kingdoms of this world, from the days of Daniel in 600 B.C. to the time of the consummation (and of course that includes us), there were to be four great universal kingdoms according to Daniel's prophecy: (1) Babylon, (2) Medo-Persia, (3) Greece, (4) Rome and thereafter. The world will never know a universal kingdom again, but it will be like the ten toes divided into iron and clay, some weak, some strong. We live in a day, not of a universal kingdom, but of strength and weakness among the nations, when nationalism is rising. And it will be thus until the days of that stone cut without hands from the mountains to fall and crush the feet of the image (Daniel 2: 34, 35). That is typical prophecy of God, who can see the end from the beginning.

The whole national life of Israel has been one of prophecy. The prophets said that God would destroy the nation (e.g. Jeremiah 15, Isaiah 15:5). Ezekiel said that God would "scatter them among the nations, and disperse them in the countries" (Ezekiel 12:15). But the prophets also said that Israel would be regathered from out of the nations to their land (Isaiah 11, 12; Ezekiel 39:27, 28). The prophets speak also of the future glory of the chosen family of God.

When He prophesied the destruction of Jerusalem in A.D. 70, and the resulting world-wide dispersement, the Lord Jesus said that this race, this genus, "this generation" will still be here when He comes again (Matthew 24:29-34). The Jew will be here, Jesus said, when He comes again. Did you ever see an Ammonite or a Canaanite or a Moabite or any other of those ancient peoples who are named in the Bible? But the Jew is still here. He is still here, and Jesus said that he will be here when He comes again.

Zechariah prophesied the word of the Lord concerning the Jews: "They shall look upon me whom they have pierced, and they shall mourn . . . as one mourneth for his only son . . . . In that day there shall be a fountain opened to the house of David . . . for sin and uncleanness" (Zechariah 12: 10, 13:1). And in Romans 11:26 Paul says that "all Israel shall be saved." Someday Israel will accept their Messiah, our Lord and Saviour.

The Bible prophesies that the mood of the world will be toward one great political configuration and confederation. The Bible predicts that there will be a movement in the world in the last times toward one great ecclesiastical confederation. You may read in your newspaper of such a movement today. The Bible speaks of the great apostasy, when men shall turn away from belief in the Word of God and from the belief that even God Himself lives.

It is not as though the Bible were telling in vague fashion of a coming Redeemer and Saviour. The prophecies are specific and detailed. There are three hundred and thirty-three precise details that describe the coming of our Lord and King—three hundred and thirty-three! In the twenty-second Psalm alone there are more than thirty exact descriptions of the cross of Jesus, written in a day when the only execution that Israel knew was stoning. Though the Psalmist spoke one thousand years before the time, it is as though he were standing by the cross.

The suffering and death of our Lord could hardly have been more poignantly described than the prophet Isaiah depicted it in the fifty-third chapter of his book:

> For he shall grow up before him as a tender plant, and as a root out of a dry ground: he hath no form nor comeliness; and when we shall see him, there is no beauty that we should desire him. He is despised and rejected of men; a man of sorrows, and acquainted with grief: and we hid as it were our faces from him; he was despised, and we esteemed him not.
>
> Surely he hath borne our griefs, and carried our sorrows: yet we did esteem him stricken, smitten of God, and afflicted. But he was wounded for our transgressions, he was bruised for our iniquities: the chastisement of our peace was upon him; and with his stripes we are healed. All we like sheep have gone astray; we have turned every one to his own way; and the Lord hath laid on him the iniquity of us all (Isaiah 53:2-6).

Isaiah wrote these words seven hundred and fifty years before Jesus died on the cross! This is the Word of God.

No wonder the incomparable prophet affirmed and the great apostle quoted, "The grass withereth, the flower fadeth: but the word of our God shall stand for ever." This is the foundation for our faith.

Chapter 3

The God-Breathed Word

> All scripture is given by inspiration of God, and is profitable for doctrine, for reproof, for correction, for instruction in righteousness: that the man of God may be perfect, throughly furnished unto all good works (II Timothy 3:16, 17).

In his second letter to Timothy, Paul reminds Timothy of the nature and purpose of the Scriptures: "All scripture is given by inspiration of God [*theopneustos,* God-breathed], and is profitable for doctrine, for reproof, for correction, for instruction in righteousness: that the man of God may be perfect [complete], throughly furnished unto all good works." (Isn't it a shame to have a chapter division between these words and the first verse of chapter 4?) "I charge thee therefore"—the "therefore" refers to the "all scripture is *theopneustos.*" "I charge thee therefore . . . preach the word."

The God-breathed Word, *theopneustos,* is exactly that—God-breathed. It is the imagery of a flute player playing his instrument by breathing into it. "All scripture is God-breathed [*theopneustos*]."

There are two words that largely characterize what God has done in writing the Bible. The first is "revelation," the second is "inspiration." Our words "revelation" and "inspiration" are basically Latin words. The Latin word meaning to uncover, unveil, reveal is *revelo.* Our word "revelation" comes from that. The Latin word meaning to breathe into is *inspiro.* Our word "inspiration" comes from that.

These words are duplicated exactly in the Greek. The Greek word meaning to unveil, uncover, make known is *apocalupto, apocalupsis* (revelation, apocalypse, uncovering). The Greek word for inspire, breathe into used in II Timothy 3:16 (and only there in the New Testament) is the one we have already referred to—*theopneustos,* meaning actually *God*-inspired. *God*-breathed. These are the words that are used to characterize what God has done in giving us the Bible.

THE DIFFERENCE BETWEEN REVELATION AND INSPIRATION

Now I want to make a distinction betwen revelation and inspiration. Revelation refers to the content. God has made known something; He has unveiled, uncovered something. Inspiration refers to the transmission of what is made known, to the method that kept it from error and mistake. To illustrate, it was an *apocalupsis,* a *revelo,* a revelation when Moses wrote the first chapter of Genesis. He was not there when God created the heavens and the earth, nor was any other man there. No human eye saw that. So it had to be made known by revelation. That is a revelation from God.

This is an inspiration: when Moses wrote, for example, of the crossing of the Red Sea, that was an inspired writing. God kept him from error, and he wrote according to the mind of the Holy Spirit. But nothing was revealed to him. Moses was writing of what he had seen with his own eyes. He had led the children of Israel through the Red Sea.

Again, to illustrate from the New Testament, it was a revelation when John wrote the Apocalypse. No man can see the consummation of the age, looking ahead thousands of years into futures known but to God. Yet God revealed that future to John, and John wrote it down. That was a revelation, an *apocalupsis.* But when John wrote, for example, the story of the crucifixion of Jesus, it was by inspiration. John was there; he saw it with his own eyes. In writing it according to the mind of the Spirit, without error or mistake and for the purpose of God, that was inspiration. Revelation refers to content. Inspiration refers to the transmission that was kept free from human error and mistake. This message is a discussion of those two—revelation and inspiration.

THE NATURE OF REVELATION

There are three assumptions that make possible a revelation from God. In the first place, we must assume that God would do it, that God can do it—that God can reveal, can uncover, can make known. The second assumption is that a man can know it, can understand it, can receive the revelation from God. And the third assumption is that the revelation pertains to something that a man in his natural, intuitive, physical power could never know. A revelation is something that only God could know, and no man could ever find out. You cannot manufacture it, you cannot discover it; it is something God has to reveal.

There are two ways that God gives a revelation. Sometimes He gives a revelation objectively. For example, it says in the Bible that God wrote the Ten Commandments with His own finger. That is an objective revelation, a revelation outside of the man himself. Another example occurs in the Book of Daniel. The finger of God wrote on the wall at Belshazzar's feast (Daniel 5). That is an objective revelation.

Or God may make the revelation subjectively. A subjective revelation is one that comes from the Spirit of God inside the man's heart and mind. For example, in II Kings 3:15 Elisha the prophet said, "Bring me a minstrel and let him play and sing for me." So while the minstrel plucked on his harp and sang, the spirit of prophecy came upon Elisha, and he spoke to the kings of Judah and Israel about what to do in the battle. The Spirit came to him in his heart. That was an inward revelation, a subjective revelation. When the finger of God wrote on the wall, that was an objective revelation. But when there came to Daniel's heart the meaning of the written words, that was subjective, intuitive revelation.

There are three characterizations of a revelation from

God. The first one is that it has progress and development. Revelation was not given all at one time. But, as the author of Hebrews wrote in the first verse of the first chapter, "God spake at sundry times and in divers manners." The revelation from God came as a river gathers its waters. Here is a tributary, there is a tributary; here is a stream, there is a stream; and finally it all is gathered together in one mighty, flowing river. So it is with the revelation of God. It was given in pieces, it was given in parts, it was given at separate times by many authors through long centuries.

As revelation continued to be given, it had movement and progress. The reason for this is very apparent, for the revelation of God in His Word was always adapted to the status of man at the time it was given. God could not speak in the youth-time of the human family for the adult period of the race. What God said in Old Testament times had to be what a man in that stage of human history could accept. Then as the progress of the human soul and the capacity of a man for God increased, so did the revelation develop and continue upward and heavenward.

A good illustration may be seen in Jesus' teaching on the subject of divorce (Matthew 19:2-13). The disciples said to the Lord, "You say that divorce is not permissible. Yet Moses, according to the law (the Old Testament), gave a writ of divorcement; the man who wanted to put away his wife wrote out that writ of divorcement and put her away. Now, why, Lord, do you say thus and so . . .?" And the Lord replied, "For the hardness of your hearts, Moses allowed such a thing"—that is, at that stage in the human family they were not able to bear the full weight of God's demands and his revelation in Jesus Christ as we know it today in the Christian dispensation.

Another instance of the progressive element in revelation may be seen in the use of force in the Old Testament and the use of moral persuasion in the New Testament as in the Sermon on the Mount. In the childhood of the race discipline and force were necessary, just as they are in the childhood of the human family. In a Sunday school class there was a bad boy misbehaving terribly. During one week, his fellow-pupils in the class attended to him. The next Sunday he was a model of excellence. So the teacher asked the other boys, "What did you say to him that he is so nice today?" The other boys said, "Well, teacher, we didn't say anything to him; we just punched him in the nose."

I heard of a small boy who was on a play horse, a little rocking horse, in a department store. His mother pleaded with the child to get off the horse as it was time to go home. The little boy would not do it. She was one of these modern mothers who had been taught that you must not lay a hand on the boy, you must not discipline him because you might warp his personality! So she just pleaded with the little boy to please get off the horse, "Please, please, pretty please, get off the horse." But he would not get off. So the manager was called, and he begged the child to get off the horse, but with no results. Then they called the psychologist, and he came and whispered something in that little boy's ear, and he got off at once. When they got home, the mother asked her son, "What did that psychologist say to you?" The little boy replied, "Mama, that psyschologist said to me, 'Listen, if you do not get off that horse right this minute I am going to beat the day-lights out of you!' "

In the younger years of the race, there were revelations and mandates of God that were fitted to that age. But as we grew older the revelation continued upward until finally it reached to the great consummation of the New Testament.

A second characteristic of revelation is that it has continuity, it has purpose, it has outreach, it is moving toward something. That which is revealed in the beginning has in it all the germinal seed of its final, ultimate consummation. For example, in the simplest mathematical axiom you have the germinal seeds and propositions of all the vast system of mathematics that is to come, including calculus and all of those Einsteinian theories that gave birth to this new modern atomic age in which we live. The ultimates are all latent; they are all enfolded in the simplest mathematical axiom.

So it is in the Word of God. Latent in those beginning revelations of the Lord are all of those ultimate consummations that we know in Christ and in the New Testament. They are enfolded in the Old Testament dispensation and unfolded in the New Testament day of grace and glory.

For example, when God gave Moses the Tabernacle, there was a purpose in the rudimentary, primary, schoolday teaching of the Tabernacle. God had to teach the human race a new language, a heavenly language. God was going to talk about atonement. He was going to talk about an altar. He was going to talk about sacrifice. He was going to talk about the expiation of our sins. But first, the race had to be taught the meaning of the language of God when He spoke of the things He was yet to work out for our redemption. So He built the Tabernacle with its meaningful furnishings and its spiritual rituals.

Now when God says "altar," I immediately know what He means by an altar. It is a place to die on. When God says the word "sacrifice," I know what He means by a sacrifice. Sacrifice is laying down your life for somebody else. I know what He means by atonement. Atonement is the spilling out of blood that washes away our sins. I know what He means by going through the veil into the presence of God and there making expiation for sins. You see, I was taught such things in the rudimentaries of God's revelation. In the seed, in the germinal revelation, there is all the latent meaning of the death of Jesus for my sins.

A third characteristic of the revelation is that it has congruity, it has inter-relatedness, it has agreement and harmony. Past is related to present, enmeshed and interconnected. And all of the parts together make up the whole revelation of God. There is one divine Mind back of the universe, and whether you are looking at gigantic Jupiter or at a microscopic paramecium, you are seeing the work of the same divine creative genius; the mind of God is stamped upon it. The Scriptures reveal the same infinite Mind. Here are the same great marks of continuity, the same great theme and subject faithfully followed and increasingly revealed through the whole Word of God.

In this connection, one may see the difference between God's way and man's way. Let's take, for example, God's theme of redemption through the whole Bible. Without variance, there is always that same presentation, that same continuity, that same inter-connectedness, that same interrelatedness, that same unvarying story. No man could write the Bible. No man would write that Bible. Only God could have conceived of the one great continual theme of redemption throughout the whole Book.

Follow, for example, the reasoning of a typical anthropologist. An anthropologist is a man who studies the human race, the beginning and origin of race, and the development of the human body. Were you to ask an anthropologist how man came to be, he would answer that back there in those primeval antiquities, in the dim mists of the past eons and ages, out of the slime and out of the dirt, a primate lifted himself up and evolved into a man. Man is the hero. He rose and rose and rose, up and up and finally one day, the anthropologist says, he will be an archangel. That would be an anthropologist's appraisal of man — a hero ascending to glory out of the slime of the earth.

But ask of God about the origin and destiny of man, and you will find His answer in His revelation. This is what God declares: man is a fallen animal, a fallen creature. Man is an abysmal, everlasting failure. He used to be perfect, set in the glory of the Eden of God. But he fell, and he fell, and he fell, and he always falls. And the only hope for the redemption of a man is in the grace of God. He can never save himself. He can never achieve heaven in himself. The grace of God must reach down and wash his sins away and regenerate his heart and make of him a new man. That is the unerring theme of the Word of God all the way through. A man is a lost creature. A man is born, he lives in iniquity and transgression, and he is lost forever except for the intervention of the goodness and grace of God and the atonement of Jesus. That is the way God looks at man.

The true preacher does not present man in any light other than that in which God shows him in His revelation. He will not stand in the pulpit to glorify hero-man. He will not seek to build another tower of Babel by which the fallen race seeks to reach to the sky and the very heavens. And yet, unfortunately, that type of message is sometimes welcomed by those who do not know God's Word or who do not desire to accept its truths.

The preacher who is faithful to his calling will stand up and look at his congregation and say that according to the Word of God and from our own experience, it is plain that we are lost sinners, and that the only way for us to find hope and life and forgiveness and salvation is in the grace of God and in the atonement of Jesus for our sins. "Come," he will say, "let us bow at the foot of the cross. Let us confess our weaknesses, our iniquities, our sins. Let us lay them all at the feet of Jesus, and let us ask God to come into our souls, into our homes, into our churches, into our nation and save our people. Our hope lies in God." Such is the message of God's true preacher.

The danger of false teaching at this point of our redemption is not to be minimized. The way of salvation is given in the revelation of God. The Scriptures never depart from the reiterated theme. Sin and atonement and the hope that lies in the grace of Jesus—these doctrines are inherent in the preaching of God's revelation.

THEORIES OF INSPIRATION

Now I come to the subject of inspiration. I have copied down from books and books and books all of the theories of inspiration that I could find. Then I sorted them into four classifications.

First, there are many theories of inspiration that I would call *rational* or radical. Let us use the word *rational,* for we have come to look upon rationalism as being a method of approach that denies a personal God and denies the supernatural. There are theories of the inspiration of the Bible that claim that the Holy Scriptures were produced by man's own intuitive powers. The Bible is denied as being supernatural, as being anything from God. According to such a theory, the authors of the Bible were inspired only in the sense that Shakespeare was inspired, that Homer was inspired, that Milton was inspired, that Tennyson was inspired, that Browning was inspired. The Bible writers were just ordinary men who occasionally rose to a little higher point of intuitive understanding than, say, Shakespeare or Homer. But they still were just ordinary men, using ordinary, intuitive, human judgments and faculties as they wrote the Bible. That is one theory of inspiration—denying a personal God, denying the supernatural, leveling the men who wrote the Bible to a par with all other men.

A second group of theories I would call *fractional* or partial. They believe that the Bible is inspired in spots. Here is an inspired passage and there is one. Here is one and there is one. The Decalogue, they would say, was inspired, but the historical section that tells about David and Goliath is a myth. They would say the twenty-third Psalm is inspired but the imprecatory Psalms are not inspired. The Bible is inspired in places. It is sectionally inspired. It contains the Word of God, but it is not the Word of God.

There is a colossal weakness in this theory because it calls for another inspiration. If the Bible is inspired in spots, somebody has to be inspired to pick out the spots so they can tell us what is inspired and what is not inspired. Foolish as it is, this theory of inspiration is most commonly accepted today.

Another theory is the *mechanical* theory. That is the persuasion that the men who wrote the Bible were just automatons. They were like dictaphones. They were like amanuenses. They were like secretaries. They just wrote down as God dictated.

Now the fourth theory, the one to which I subscribe, explains to my satisfaction how God has given us the Holy Bible in revelation without error or mistake. I believe in a *dynamic, plenary, verbal, supernatural* presentation of the writing of the Holy Book. It is *dynamic* in the sense that God empowered the personalities and minds and experiences and hearts of men to do it. It is *plenary* in the sense that all of it, all of the scripture is *theopneustos,* all of it is God-breathed. And it is *verbal* in the sense that every jot and tittle of it is inspired. It is *supernatural* in the sense that it comes from God and has a supernatural effect upon those who receive its message and believe its Christ.

Now let us consider these four aspects of the writing of the Bible in detail.

First, it is *dynamic.* As I have said, by that I mean that God empowers men, the minds of men, the personalities of men, the hearts and souls of men, the experiences of men, to write the Book. The Bible is not alien to a man's intelligence or to his human reception and understanding. It is something that a man can read and know and understand. It is written that we might be intelligent Christians and disciples of our Lord. When God made the prophets, when God made the apostles, He did not un-make the man. The writer is still a man. He is still Peter or Paul or David or Moses. When the bush burned unconsumed, it was still a bush. When the Lord sent a raven to feed Elijah, it was still a raven. And when God said He ordained praise out of the mouths of babes and sucklings, they had to remain babes and sucklings or the imagery and prophecy of God is of no effect. So God uses in a dynamic, *theopneustos,* "God-breathed" way the personality of the man who writes.

There is the conjoining of the human and the divine in the author. This can be seen most vividly in the personality of Christ. He is both man and God. This can be experienced in our own regeneration. The human and the divine work together in our salvation. There was a part in our salvation we played; there was a part in our salvation that God played. Both divine and human meet in all that God does in this world.

George Eliot wrote a poem about Antonio Stradivarius in which she represents the famous Italian violin-maker as saying,

> If my hand slacked
> I should rob God
> Since He is fullest good,
> Leaving a blank
> Instead of violins.
> God cannot make
> Antonio Stradivarius violins
> Without Antonio.

God uses the man, breathes upon the man. Yet every man retains his own personality, his own approach, his own language, his own idiosyncrasies and styles. Isaiah was a brilliant court-preacher, and he spoke in highflown, glorious alliterations and perorations. Amos was a country preacher, and when you read his talks and prophecies, they smell of a new-plowed furrow, of the dirt and the soil. For God to have placed in the mouth of Amos the highflown literary language of Isaiah would have been incongruous. So Amos speaks as a farmer would speak, and Isaiah speaks as a brilliant court-preacher would speak. But both of them are God-breathed, God using their personalities. Thus it is always in God's use of men.

Christmas Evans had one good eye. The other one was out. And I do not know how many times that piercing luminous eye was used of God to bring sinners to repentance. Dwight L. Moody was very ungrammatical in his messages. But God baptized that lack of grammar in Moody and made him a tremendous soul-winner. Phillips Brooks was a chaste and polished Bostonian preacher. Sam Jones was a humorist, and he cut with that two-edged sword with devastating effect. Billy Sunday ran baseball bases in the pulpit. God uses the personality of the man, and adapts it to the form of the revelation that He gives to him.

Moses as the heir to the throne of Egypt was trained in all of the law and background of the Egyptians. And in the law of Moses you will find reflected that marvelous training. Paul was trained in rabbinical casuistry and hair-splitting theology, and this background is reflected here in this letter he wrote to Timothy. David was a sweet psalmist, the sweet singer of Israel, as evidenced in the beautiful songs that he wrote. And Solomon was a wise man, whose wisdom is seen in the proverbs he wrote. So the whole Bible has the dynamic of God in it, as God used the mind and soul and personality of each author.

THE PLENARY INSPIRATION OF THE WORD OF GOD

A second thing about this theory of inspiration to which I humbly subscribe is the *plenary* inspiration of the Bible. All of it is inspired. Now there are degrees of value. There are degrees of worth in the Bible. But there are not degrees of inspiration. I may not find as much worth in the catalog of genealogies as I do in the Sermon on the Mount or in the story of the death of Christ. But one is as inspired as the other. It takes it all to make the Book complete. And there are no degrees in completeness. This is complete in its part; that is complete in its part; and both are true. When we put it all together, it makes the whole revelation complete. I believe in the *plenary* inspiration of the Scriptures. All of it is inspired of God. The fallible men may have passed away, but the infallible words that they delivered abide forever.

I believe in the *verbal* inspiration of the Bible. Our Lord said that "not a jot [not a dotting of an 'i'], not a tittle [not the crossing of a 't'] shall pass away from the law until all be fulfilled." I believe in the jot and in the tittle, in the very words that are used in the Holy Bible to reveal the great disclosure of God to us. Let me say it like this: you cannot have mathematics without figures; you cannot have thoughts without words. And when those thoughts are inspired, the words by which God expressed them are part of that same inspired revelation. This is the basis for all exegesis. The man who preaches the Bible and expounds the Word of God is going on the assumption that that Word is *theopneustos,* inspired by God breathing into the mind and the soul, objectively and subjectively portraying His revelation from heaven.

Finally, the Bible is a *supernatural* revelation. It is a gift from heaven. God pulled back the veil that hides Him from us. He speaks to us, He reveals to us, He uncovers to us, He makes known to us His will both now and into the forevers. The revelation is from heaven. No *man* can unveil the future and look ahead. To do so is supernatural. It is beyond what a man could ever know or ever discover, however enlightened his intuitive faculties to know the future. This knowledge comes from God.

The Bible is supernatural in its divine and heavenly effect upon those who hear its message and receive its words; they are transported and translated into the kingdom of everlasting life and glory. It is supernatural in its divine effect upon the human soul and the human family.

When I was a pastor in a little country church, one of the godly deacons, a farmer, fell heir some way to a Spanish Bible. He could not read a word of it and wondered what to do with it. Then he remembered that in the community was a Mexican family. He made his way up to the house and knocked at the door and was greeted by the father of the large family. The deacon said: "I have a gift for you, a Bible. It is written in Spanish, in your language. I am giving it to you." The Mexican took it with gratitude, saying, *"Gracias, gracias."*

One day when the farmer had forgotten the incident, there was a knock at his door. There stood that Mexican tenant farmer. He said, "You know the Book you gave us? We have been reading the Book and we have all been saved.

We have accepted Jesus as our Saviour. And it says in the Book that we ought to be baptized, and I have come to ask if I and all of my family could be baptized." They brought the matter to me. I said, "We rejoice, we thank God." So I baptized the Mexican and his large family.

Then one day a fire broke out in the tenant farmer's house. As the house was going up in flames, the farmers who had gathered around to watch saw that Mexican dash into those burning embers and come back out with the Bible. He had rescued from the flames the Word of God and held it in his hands, a treasure forever. Scripture is supernatural in its effect upon the human soul.

Such is the Book of God. "The grass withereth, the flower fadeth but the word of our Lord," inspired, plenarily, verbally, dynamically, supernaturally, "abides in glory and in power forever."

Chapter 4

Christ and the Prophets

> Then he said unto them, O fools, and slow of heart to believe all that the prophets have spoken: Ought not Christ to have suffered these things, and to enter into his glory? And beginning at Moses and all the prophets, he expounded unto them in all the scriptures the things concerning himself. . . . And he said unto them, These are the words which I spake unto you, while I was yet with you, that all things must be fulfilled, which were written in the law of Moses, and in the prophets, and in the psalms, concerning me. Then opened he their understanding, that they might understand the scriptures, and said unto them, Thus it is written, and thus it behoved Christ to suffer, and to rise from the dead the third day: and that repentance and remission of sins should be preached in his name among all nations, beginning at Jerusalem (Luke 24:25-27, 44-47).

Let me speak first of the attestations to, the authentications and corroborations of the truth of our most holy and sacred faith. One could elaborate endlessly on his persuasion that the things that we believe in Christ are eternally and everlastingly true. One could refer to the perfect life of our Lord. No other faith, no other religion has a Jesus, our Christ. One could speak of the effect of the Christian religion upon the people who receive it and believe it and adore our living Lord.

But what is the greatest and highest of all of the attestations that Christ is truly the Son of God, the one used by Jesus Himself and by the apostles? In the New Testament the chief of all of the attestations to the truth of the Christian faith is this: fulfillment of the Old Testament prophecies concerning things that came to pass in the life and ministry of our Lord. The great corroboration that God was in Christ, reconciling the world unto Himself, is found in this: that He fulfilled the prophecies of the Old Testament.

That the ministry of our Lord was in fulfillment of Old Testament prophecy is very typically illustrated in our Saviour's conversation with the two on the road to Emmaus. Jesus had said He would rise from the dead but His disciples had forgotten His Word. These two were amazingly skeptical of the report of some women who said they had seen Him risen. They had watched Him crucified and had come to the conclusion that this was the end of the ministry and mission of their hoped-for Saviour. So when Christ, unknown to them, a stranger to them (for not until He had revealed Himself in opening their eyes did they recognize Him), sought to bring them to an undying and everlasting faith in Himself, how did He do it? Did He work some marvelous miracle before the eyes of those two disciples who were so discouraged and in such despair? Did He corroborate the truth of His life and resurrection by fire from heaven? Did He do some wondrous, spectacular thing? Did He even remind them of His words of wisdom and of the glory of the days of His flesh? No! What He did was this: out of the Old Testament Scriptures, "beginning at Moses and all the prophets, he expounded unto them in all the scriptures the things concerning himself." The great corroboration and attestation and proof of the ministry of our Lord He found in the Holy Scriptures themselves.

That same attitude and presentation prevail in the work and writing and preaching of the apostles. The gospel of Matthew is none other than a presentation of our Lord as the fulfillment of all of the prophecies of the Old Testament. Time and again will you find in Matthew this formula: this was done or this happened "that it might be fulfilled which was spoken by the prophet." Simon Peter in his sermon at Caesarea said of Jesus, "To him give all the prophets witness." When the eloquent Alexandrian, Apollos, spoke in Ephesus, the Bible says that "he mightily convinced the

Jews, and that publicly, showing by the scriptures that Jesus was Christ" (Acts 18:28). In his great letter to the church at Corinth Paul defined the gospel:

> I declare unto you, I make known unto you, the gospel wherein ye are saved, how that Christ died for our sins according to the scriptures, that he was buried and the third day he rose again according to the scriptures (I Corinthians 15:1, 4).

To summarize: In the New Testament the tremendous corroboration of faith in Jesus Christ is this: that he fulfilled Old Testament prophecy.

THE MIRACLE OF PROPHECY

Now I speak of the merit and the worth and the glory of that attestation. From about A.D. 100 to 165 there lived a converted philosopher in Samaria. He was a Greek, a learned rhetorician. His name was Justin, and because he laid down his life for the faith, history knows him as Justin Martyr. How did this Greek intellectual become a convert to the Christian faith? By reading the Old Testament Scriptures and finding their fulfillment in Jesus Christ.

Let me quote a sentence from the testimony of this great Christian witness: "To declare a thing shall come to pass long before it is in being, and then to bring it to pass, this or nothing is the work of God." The marvelous faith of that Greek philosopher as he read the Old Testament Scriptures and prophecies and found them fulfilled in Jesus the Christ, is the marvelous faith that will come to any honest heart who will read God's Word and who will find those holy prophecies fulfilled in our blessed Lord.

To know the future is a prerogative of God alone. No man can foresee the future; not a minute hence, not a day hence, much less a thousand years hence. No man can know the future but God. And for God to outline the future and to bring it to pass as He has written it, is a work and a miracle and an attestation of the presence and truth of the Lord God Himself.

If a mere man were to prophecy that a hundred years

hence or a thousand years hence, there would be somebody such as he describes come to live in the earth, the fulfillment would be a phenomenal, a marvelous thing. But in the Bible not just one man at one particular time foretells and prophesies the coming to the earth of another man. Many men through many centuries spoke concerning the coming to this earth of a great Personality, a great Man. Not only did they say He was coming, but they intimately described a multitude of details concerning Him.

How long ago was it, in a time known but to God, that He created Adam and Eve in the Garden of Eden? And after their fall, how long ago was it that God promised that by the seed of the woman (a prophecy of the virgin birth of the coming Saviour) Satan would be crushed? How long ago was that? The prophecies follow through the days of Abraham, two thousand years before Christ. They are uttered in the time of Moses, one thousand and four hundred years before Christ. They occur in the lifetime of Jacob, the third after Abraham. They continue in David's time, a thousand years before Christ; in the utterances of Isaiah, seven hundred and fifty years before Christ; in the Book of Micah, seven hundred years before Christ. The prophets are speaking in intimate detail of the great coming One, the promised of God.

Pascal, one of the greatest scientific minds of all time and one of the most influential, wrote these meaningful words: "The greatest of the proofs of Jesus Christ are the prophecies. They are also what God has most provided for, for the event which has fulfilled them is a miracle of God." The observation of Pascal is eminently true. It is astonishing that men, under the Holy Spirit of God, should outline and foretell the life of our Lord in minutest detail. The fifty-third chapter of Isaiah, for example, written over seven hundred and fifty years before Christ, reads as though a man had stood by the cross of the Son of God himself.

No less a miraculous part of those prophecies, delivered under the inspiration of God, is that they seemingly contradict one another. For that reason, until they were fulfilled in our Lord, no man could untangle them. At one time the prophet would picture the coming One as a great conqueror. In the next breath, the same prophet might describe His lowliness and sorrow and grief. How could that be? Here was a great conqueror, riding triumphant as leader of the nations of the earth, but lowly and despised and outcast, a man of sorrows and acquainted with grief. In one breath the prophets would present Him as the King of Heaven, the King of Glory, the King of the nations, the desire of all the peoples of the earth. In the next they would describe His stripes, His blood, and His atoning death. How could those things be? Even John the Baptist did not understand. He sent his disciples to our Lord to inquire whether or not there were two Christs, one to be the Lamb of God, the suffering Saviour, and the other to be the Judge of all the earth, burning the chaff with unquenchable fire. The diverse and apparently contradictory prophecies and their fulfillment constitute the greatest attestation of the Christian faith that mind could imagine. These things God had written thousands of years before they found their explanation in the life of our Lord.

THE PROPHECIES FULFILLED IN JESUS

Now we come to the second part of our message. Can we be sure that those prophecies were actually fulfilled in Jesus? The Hebrew people, of course, disavow it, disown it, repudiate it. Are we sure that all of these things written by the Spirit of God in the Old Testament Scriptures are fulfilled in Jesus Christ? Unbelievers might rise up and say, "Now before you stand up there and declare that these prophecies in the Old Tetstament are fulfilled in Jesus Christ, we have three objections." All right, let us listen to their objections.

First, they might say that Jesus apparently fulfilled those Old Testament Scriptures because there was collusion between Jesus and His friends to make the life of our Lord conform to all of those Old Testament prophecies, that it was planned, that it was a trick, and we are dupes to believe it. Why is that objection not valid? For the simple and plain reason that most of the predictions that were made about the life of our Lord were not fulfilled by the friends of Jesus or by the acts of Jesus Himself. They were fulfilled by His enemies, who hated Him and who slew Him. Who broke the bones of those malefactors on each side of His cross but failed to break His bones? Who did that? Were they the friends of Jesus who came and broke the bones of the thief on one side and the thief on the other side? Or were they the men who crucified Him? They were the men who crucified Him. But the Scriptures had said a bone of His would not be broken. "And when they came to Jesus [the center cross], and saw that He was dead already, they brake not his legs" (John 19:33).

The Scriptures also had said a thousand years before He died that Israel would look on the one whom they had pierced (Zechariah 12:10). John records that "one of the soldiers with a spear pierced his side and forthwith came there out blood and water" (John 19:34).

I am just illustrating the fact that many of the Scriptures that prophesy the life and ministry of our Lord were not fulfilled by His friends. They were fulfilled by those who hated Him and finally destroyed and crucified Him. So there could not have been a collusion between Jesus and His friends to make His life conform to the prophecies of the Old Testament.

Then the skeptics have another avowal. They say that friends of Jesus wrote those prophecies in the Old Testament Scriptures. Then when the life of Jesus followed its course, they had already changed the Scriptures to conform to His life. The answer to that is very apparent. The Old Testament Scriptures were as set, as well-known, as infallible, as sacred to the Jew when Jesus lived as they are to the Jew and to us today. The Old Testament canon was completed after the days of Ezra, and the books were completely translated into Greek (forming the Septuagint) about three hundreds years before Christ. For the apostles to have tried to change those Scriptures to make them conform to the life of our Lord would have been utterly impossible.

There are thousands of scholars today, besides the ordinary believer who is listening to me out there in the pew, who would know it if a man changed the Bible, the Word of God. It was likewise so in the days of our Lord. For hundreds of years before Christ was born, those Scriptures were canonized, they were set, they were known and studied, they were definitely transcribed according to a certain pattern. Every page had its letter in a certain place, quite different from what it is now because today we have many different versions and translations. Every copy of those Hebrew Scriptures in that day when our Lord lived, however, was exactly like every other copy. Every letter was identically transcribed onto the same spot on every page. For the apostles or the friends of Jesus to have changed those Scriptures would have been utterly impossible.

There is one other objection, namely, that the fulfillment of those prophetic Scriptures may refer not to Jesus but to some other man. Plainly written in the pages of the Old Testament is a description of the coming One, what He is to be like, what He is to do. Could it refer to someone other than Jesus? To Socrates? To Plato? To Caesar? To Marcus Aurelius? To Alexander the Great? To Charlemagne? To Napoleon? In our own day there have been men of stature such as Winston Churchill, as great as any in the ages past. But who would in wildest imagination ever think of identifying a Winston Churchill as the fulfillment of the prophecies of God? For those who lived in the days of Socrates, or of Plato, or of Charlemagne, or of Alexander, or of Caesar, it would have been as impossible, it would have been as unthinkable to identify one of those men as the fulfillment of the Messianic prophecies of the Old Testament Scriptures. There is just one Christ. There is only one, and His name is Jesus. All of those multitudinous descriptions and prophecies put together constitute an outline of the life, ministry, birth, death, resurrection, ascension, and coming again of our living and glorious Lord.

THE GRIEVOUS SIN OF UNBELIEF

To conclude, it is because this truth is so evident that the sin of unbelief is so grievous and, if persisted in, becomes what the Book would call the unpardonable sin. The Father has authenticated Jesus as only God in heaven could do: "This is my beloved Son, . . . hear ye him" (Matthew 17:5). The Bible has authenticated Jesus, our Saviour, as the Christ of God. For a man to persist in rejection and unbelief becomes an unforgivable, eternal and unpardonable sin.

God forgives the harlot. One came off the street, out of the gutter, and bathed His feet with her tears, dried His feet with the hair of her head, and the Lord lifted her out and sent her away in forgiveness and in peace. The Lord forgives the harlot. The Lord forgives the malefactor, the traitor and the murderer. Dying, one of them turned and looked to Jesus, saying, "Lord, when you come into your kingdom, remember me" (Luke 23:42). There is one man I know is in heaven. He was a thief and a murderer, guilty of insurrection. For the Lord said to that repentant thief, "To day [this day, *semeron,* not at the resurrection, not at the age of consummation, but today, this very day] shalt thou be with me in paradise" (Luke 23:43). When the Lord entered into glory, He did not come in by Himself but arm-in-arm with a converted outcast. "Lift up your heads, O ye gates . . . and the King of glory shall come in" (Psalm 24:7), and when He came in, by His side came a repentant murderer, insurrectionist, robber, thief.

God will forgive the thief. God will forgive us when we deny our Lord. Simon Peter cursed and swore and said: "You think I talk like Him? Then listen to this!" (Matthew 26:73, 74). While he was cursing, the Lord turned and looked upon Peter, "and he went out and wept bitterly." The Lord later appeared especially to Simon Peter to encourage him in the reality of the divine mercy. There is not any sin God will not forgive, not any sin.

But, "he that believeth not is condemned already" (John 3:18). The unbeliever is judged, cast out, refused as unworthy, for God has done all that God could do to attest, to verify, to authenticate the saving mission of His Son. "This is my beloved Son . . . hear ye him" (Matthew 17:5). Oh, that this could be the day of our avowal of faith and of the commitment of our lives to Jesus!

Our Lord, on trial for His life, spoke under oath before the high priest. The high priest had said to Jesus, "I adjure thee by the living God, that thou tell us whether thou be the Christ, the Son of God" (Matthew 26:63). Before the Sanhedrin presided over by the high priest, and under oath, the Lord replied, "I am [I am the Christ of God]: and ye shall see the Son of man sitting on the right hand of power and coming in the clouds of heaven" (Mark 14:62).

> When He shall come with trumpet sound,
> Oh, may I then in Him be found;
> Dressed in His righteousness alone,
> Faultless to stand before the throne.
> On Christ, the solid rock, I stand;
> All other ground is sinking sand,
> All other ground is sinking sand.

In the light of that attestation and on the firm rock of that avowal, the apostles preached, the martyrs testified and the true Church of Jesus rises today to proclaim her Lord as the hope of the world.

"And beginning at Moses and all the prophets, he expounded unto them in all the scriptures the things concerning himself." Heaven's highest attestation is the witness of the Word of God.

Chapter 5

The Word God Has Spoken

> And the king of Israel said unto his servants, Know ye that Ramoth in Gilead is ours, and we be still, and take it not out of the hand of the king of Syria? (I Kings 22:3).

In the twenty-second chapter of I Kings there is recounted one of the most unusually interesting stories to be found in all literature. King Ahab of Israel said to King Jehoshaphat of Judah: "Ramoth in Gilead, across the Jordan River, belongs to us. Let us take it from the hand of those heathen." That pleased Jehoshaphat and he said, "My heart is with yours." So they joined their armies together in preparation for an invasion of Gilead.

Then Jehoshaphat said, "Let us inquire at the mouth of the Lord." So King Ahab of Israel called together four hundred of his prophets and asked them, "What does God say about this campaign against Ramoth-Gilead?" "Oh," they all said, "the Lord says, 'Go up and take it. I will deliver it into your hands.' "

But Jehoshaphat hesitated and finally said to Ahab, "Is there not one other prophet of Jehovah from whom we might inquire?" Ahab replied, "Yes, there is, but I hate him." Jehoshaphat said: "Let not the king say so. Bring him before us that we might inquire the word of the Lord from him."

So Micaiah was brought before the king and they asked him, "Micaiah, what does God say, what is the word of the Lord?" Micaiah answered, "I saw a vision of Israel scattered like sheep upon a hill without a shepherd." That was his way of saying, "You go up against Gilead and the army will be defeated and the king will be slain."

Then Zedekiah, who was the leader of the four hundred other prophets who were purporting to deliver the Word of the Lord, went over to Micaiah and in contempt slapped him on his cheek and said, "How was it and when, that the Spirit of God and the Word of the Lord departed from me and went to you?" And Micaiah, the prophet of God, said, "You will see it in the day when you hide yourself in your chamber in shame."

Then Ahab said to his bodyguards, "Take that Micaiah and put him in prison and feed him bread of affliction and water of affliction until I come again in triumph and victory." But Micaiah answered, "If you come again at all the Lord hath not spoken by me."

So the two kings went against Ramoth-Gilead. In the battle an archer drew back his bow at a venture, never aiming, and let fly an arrow that found a joint in the harness of King Ahab. It went through his heart and his blood spilled out on the floor of the chariot. They brought him back to Jezreel dead and washed out the chariot by the pool of Jezreel and the dogs licked up his blood, "according to the saying of the man of God." That is the background.

How Can We Know the True Word of God?

The center of that story revolves around the question, What is the Word of God? How do you know this is the Book of God? There are many books that purport to be God's Book. There are many statements that purport to be what God said. How do you test the Word of God and what are the criteria, the testings of the Word of God? How do you recognize it?

Let us turn to the Book itself. Out of a multitude of tests that we could follow, I have chosen three criteria that are mentioned here in this sacred volume on how you can tell that it is the Word of God.

The first one is in Deuteronomy 18:21, 22:

> And if thou say in thine heart, How shall we know the word which the Lord hath not spoken? When a prophet speaketh in the name of the Lord, if the thing follow not, nor come to pass, that is the thing which the Lord hath not spoken, but the prophet hath spoken it presumptuously: thou shalt not be afraid of him.

The first test when a man makes a prophecy, according to the Word of the Lord, is whether it comes to pass. Is he able to prophesy? Is he able to foretell the future?

That is a far more significant and difficult test than you realize. Did you know that there is no other religion on earth that has a prophet except the Bible religion, the Judeo-Christian faith? Did you know there is no such thing as prophecy in any other religion on earth except our religion? Why? For the simple reason that only God can foresee the future and only God can prophesy. It is not in the power of man to do it.

Prophecy is not to be confused with such predictions as a survey or a poll forecast, or the sort of "tip" that may be made concerning what horse will win a race. A poll may show that a certain candidate will be elected, but it is by no means sure that he will be. Were the horse to win that is supposed to do so according to a prediction, someone would make a fortune; but actually there is no way of knowing beforehand within the power of a human being, unless, of course, the race is "fixed." Playing the stock market can be financially disastrous or it can be richly rewarding, depending upon how right a "hunch" may prove to be. There is nothing certain about predictions made by man when such forecasts are the result of his own thinking. But prophecy is above these man-made forecasts; it is certain of fulfillment because it is from God.

Eight hundred years before Christ a humble prophet named Micah said, "The Lord is coming and He is going to be born in a little town named Bethlehem." When the time came Mary and Joseph lived in Nazareth, not Bethlehem. But eight hundred years earlier Micah had said that the Messiah was going to be born in Bethlehem.

"In those days," eight hundred years after Micah's prophecy, "there went out a decree from Caesar Augustus [in the imperial city of Rome], that all the world should be taxed [enrolled]" (Luke 2:1). There was to be a universal census. The emperor never dreamed that he was fulfilling the prophecy of God made eight hundred years before. So Joseph and his wife, she being heavy with child, made that solemn journey down to the city of Bethelehem, that it might be fulfilled which was spoken by Micah the prophet, "In Bethlehem shall he be born who shall be ruler in Israel."

When they nailed Jesus to a tree, He was crucified by a quaternion of soldiers under a centurion. As the custom was in the Roman day of crucifixion, the clothing of the criminal was divided among the soldiers. One of the soldiers took His turban, one took His outer garment, another took His girdle, and the fourth soldier took His sandals. But there was one garment left, the fifth, His inner garment, woven without seam from top to bottom. And the soldiers said, "Let's not tear it and divide it into four parts. Let's cast lots for it and see who gets it." Thus they fulfilled "that which was spoken by the prophet" one thousand years before, when David said, "They divide my garments among them, and for my raiment they cast lots" (Psalm 22:18, RSV). One thousand years before!

After Jesus died, those same soldiers went to the malefactor who died on His left and broke his legs. Then they went to the one who died on His right and broke his legs. When they came to Jesus in the center they did not break His legs, but one of the soldiers took a spear and thrust it into His side. When they ruptured His heart, blood and water flowed out, "that it might be fulfilled which was spoken by the prophet" one thousand, four hundred years before, "A bone of him shall not be broken" (John 19:31-37; Psalm 34:20); and that it might be fulfilled which was spoken by the prophet Zechariah, five hundred and twenty

years before, "and they shall look upon me whom they have pierced" (Zechariah 12:10).

Thousands of years, hundreds of years in advance God has prophesied things that have since come to pass. This is the first test of the true Word of God. Man cannot tell the future three minutes from now, but God reveals the future thousands of years hence. He sees the end from the beginning.

The second test I have chosen is in Psalm 119:160: "Thy word is true from the beginning: and every one of thy righteous judgments endureth for ever." The second criterion is that the Book be without error. "Thy word is true from the beginning."

The Lord God, who made all of creation, understands it. We are just now learning about it. Jet propulsion has been here from the beginning of creation. But we are just learning to use it. The waves that bear the sound of radio and on which the words and pictures ride in television were here from the beginning. It is just now that we are discovering them. And the Lord God, who made these things and spoke of these things, is the One who understands them from the beginning of creation. If the Bible speaks about them in error, it is not the Word of God. But the Holy Scriptures say, "Thy word is true from the beginning." God, who knows all things, would not make an error in describing the world that He created.

THE FAMOUS TRIAL OF THE WORD OF GOD IN NEW YORK CITY

Here is an illustration of that truth. This is the strangest thing that ever happened, I think, in the history of jurisprudence. On the thirty-first day of October, 1939, the following notice appeared in the *Herald Tribune* in New York City: "Rev. Harry Rimmer speaks nightly this week and Sunday at the Central Baptist Church, 92nd Street and Amsterdam Avenue on 'The Harmony of Science and Scripture.' He offers $1,000 for a scientific error in the Bible."

He publicly offered $1,000 to anyone who could point out a scientific error in the Bible.

A Mr. William Floyd read this and demanded the money, alleging a number of scientific errors in the Bible. Since he could not prove that they were scientific errors to the satisfaction of the preacher and the church, he entered suit in the courts of New York City against both the preacher and the Central Baptist Church. This is the only time such a thing has ever happened in the history of the world. The trial was held in New York City on the fifteenth day of February, 1940. The plaintiff brought in four witnesses besides himself to establish his case: Rabbi Baruch Bronstein of an ultra-liberal Hebrew Synagogue; Rev. John Haynes Holmes, pastor of the Community Church; Rev. Charles Francis Potter, pastor of the First Humanist Church; Mr. Woolsey Teller, Vice-President of the American Association for the Advancement of Atheism; all of them of New York City. So the trial got underway. The skeptics proposed to prove in court the scientific errors in the Bible in order to collect that $1,000 from the preacher who was preaching at the Central Baptist Church.

The first witness to come before the court was the plaintiff. One of the things he majored on was Numbers 11:31, 32 which describes the quail the Lord sent to give flesh to the murmuring Israelites on their journey through the wilderness. And this is the passage in Numbers 11:31, 32:

> And there went forth a wind from the Lord, and brought quails from the sea, and let them fall by the camp, as it were a day's journey on this side, and as it were a day's journey on the other side, round about the camp, and as it were two cubits high upon the face of the earth. And the people stood up all that day, and all that night, and all the next day, and they gathered the quails: and he that gathered least gathered ten homers.

The plaintiff figured that this meant a deposit of quail about four feet deep, covering all the surface of the earth for three thousand one hundred and thirty-six square miles. Then he continued and I quote from him directly:

> The cubical content of this mass of quail would be approximately three hundred five billion, two hundred fifty-eight million, five hundred fifty-two thousand, four hundred forty-eight cubit feet of quail, estimating that each quail pressed in the mass would occupy about three inches by three inches of space, thus displacing some twenty-seven cubit inches of space per quail in the pile. The total number of quail, therefore, in this mass or mess of quail would be nineteen trillion, five hundred thirty-eight billion, four hundred sixty-eight million, three hundred six thousand, six hundred and seventy-two quail presented to the eye of the fundamentalist faith.

That is what he proposed to the court.

There was a fatal defect in his testimony, however, in that he did not know Hebrew. Actually, the Holy Scriptures say that God blew the quail into the wilderness from the Nile Valley, and the sense of the original text is that "they were [flying] above the face of the earth about two cubits." Not that they were pressed down and packed together like sardines in a can, but that they were flying close to the earth. It was very easy, then, for the people to catch them with their hands or knock them down with a stick. That is all God said in His Book. So the judge dismissed the ineffectual witness.

The second witness was brought in, Rabbi Bronstein. He started off by saying: "I am a member of the liberal wing of the Hebrew faith. I am a scholar and I have read a great deal." He said that the Bible contradicts itself as to the number of animals taken into the ark, saying in one place there were two of a kind and in another place seven of each kind.

The Honorable James E. Bennett, counsel for the defense, cross-examined him. Bennett turned to Genesis 7:2 and said to the Rabbi, "Read this verse out loud." So the Rabbi read: "And the Lord said unto Noah . . . Of every clean beast thou shalt take to thee by sevens, the male and his female: and of beasts that are not clean by two, the male and his female." The Rabbi then said, "Well, I now think I am mistaken. I now believe the Bible is correct." So he turned out to be a witness for the defense, and the judge dismissed him.

They brought in next Rev. John Haynes Holmes, pastor of the Community Church in New York City. Under questioning, he admitted that he did not know anything about science, that is, he was not an authority on science, and he admitted that his ideas concerning the Biblical account of creation were merely his own opinions, that he could not qualify to speak for anyone else. That did not constitute legal evidence, so the judge dismissed him.

The next witness was Charles Francis Potter, pastor of the First Humanist Church in New York City, who stated that no such thing had ever happened like the flood as described in Genesis. The judge asked the witness if he had been there, and if not, where he got his information that there was no such thing as a flood. The witness said that he got his information from superficial reading and he finally admitted that his opinions were just his own. The shrewd lawyer, Mr. James Bennett, made that preacher admit under cross-examination that he did not know whether or not there was a God since he was an agnostic and ignorant on that subject. The preacher admitted that he had never prayed and that he thought the idea of God was just a figment in some people's mind. The judge dismissed him.

The next witness was the Vice-President for the American Association for the Advancement of Atheism, Woolsey Teller. He appeared the next day, on Friday the sixteenth of February in 1940, and he really had a lot to say. He repeated all of those atheistic criticisms that have been made against the Bible, the Word of God, from the days of Celsus to Voltaire to Ingersoll to 1940. He claimed to be an accredited scientist, to be liberally educated in theology with answers for everything ecclesiastical. But under cross-examination, he had to admit that he had never been to college and that all he knew he had learned from reading magazines and articles and infidel books. When they continued to cross-examine that atheist, they compelled him to admit the pseudo-scientific monstrosities that have been pawned off as being the true and the infallible findings of research.

One of the men that this atheist had used for an authority was the famous Dr. Fairfield Osborn of the American Museum of Natural History, one of America's great paleontologists and one of the great anthropologists of the world. The lawyer for the defense was a very able lawyer. He began his questioning by saying,

> Now I see that you cite here as one of your great anthropological and paleontological authorities, Dr. Fairfield Osborn, and you quote him as being one of those so-called infallible men. He gives judgments on the research of science that have assured results. I want to ask you about one thing that this Fairfield Osborn did.

Then he went on to say that some time previously there had been discovered a tooth in Nebraska by a Mr. Harold Cook, which had been named *Hespero-Pithicus.* It belonged to a western ape-man (that is what *Hespero-Pithicus* means — western ape-man). The scientists took that tooth, and around it they built an ape-man, the missing link between the anthropoid and the Homo-sapiens, between us and the animal. They built a man around that tooth, and they built a female around that tooth, and then they built a whole race around that tooth. They even built the habitat and the culture and the rude civilization of this ape-man, this *Hespero-Pithicus,* who was supposed to have covered this continent over one million years ago.

That so-called scientific evidence was used in the Scopes trial in Dayton, Tennessee. Clarence Darrow used it to flail William Jennings Bryan. Bryan answered: "I don't know what to say. You say because of that tooth there was an anthropoid man, an ape-man, a *Hespero-Pithicus,* who lived here a million years ago. I don't know what to say. So let's wait for more evidence." They laughed and ridiculed William Jennings Bryan then. Had not the great Dr. Fairfield Osborn and his fellow-anthropologists reconstructed the whole life of these ape-people? But in the years since the trial they had found the skeleton of the animal to whom that tooth belonged. It turned out to be a peccary, a wild hog that used to roam the mid-continent of America a long, long time ago.

When the defense lawyer and Mr. Teller got to talking about those things, the trial grew so ridiculous that the judge threw the case out of court and ended it. It has never been mentioned since.

My young friends, whoever you are and wherever you are studying, when you assume that God does not know what He is talking about, when you say that God made scientific errors in this Book, and when you seek to point them out and to prove them, you have troubles on your hands. There has never lived a man yet who was smarter than God. That second criterion in testing the Holy Bible is powerful. There are no errors in the manuscripts of God. "Thy word is true from the beginning: and every one of thy righteous judgments endureth for ever" (Psalm 119: 160).

THE PURPOSE OF THE HOLY SCRIPTURES

There is a third criterion by which we can examine the Word of God. The first one is that the Bible has in it prophecy which comes to pass. The second one is that the Word of God is without error. The third one is that the Word of God accomplishes its purpose. "For," said Isaiah,

> as the rain cometh down, and the snow from heaven, and returneth not thither . . . so shall my word be that goeth forth out of my mouth: it shall not return unto me void, but it shall accomplish that which I please, and it shall prosper in the thing whereto I sent it (55:10, 11).

God's Word does for God what He has willed for it.

Now, what does God will for His Word? The Bible is not a book of geology. It was not intended to be. It is not a book of chemistry. God did not write it for that purpose. It is not a book of astronomy. It has nothing to do with any of these things that enter into the modern, scientific research. The purpose of God's Word is that we might someday see His face and live, that we might be delivered from the penalty and the judgment of our sins.

All of us are under condemnation. All of us are fallen. All of us face death. All of us face the Judgment. And when a man faces death and the Judgment, what shall he do and where shall he turn and what shall he say? God's Book is written that we might be redeemed, that we might be saved, that we might know the name of the Lord, that someday we might live with Him in a higher and better world that is yet to come. Does the Bible accomplish its purpose? Is God able to deliver us?

In one of England's industrial cities, in a great mill complex, an atheist was standing up haranguing the millworkers about the inaccuracies of the Bible and the myths and the fables in the Word of God. "All of this story about Jesus and all those things about the Lord in the Bible are just fables and myths and legends." While he was talking, an old unlettered, ignorant millhand stood up and said, "May I ask you a question?" The atheist answered, "Yes." "Until recently I was a vile sinner," said the millhand. "I was a curse to myself and a curse to my family and a curse to all who knew me. Then I heard the blessed story of Jesus and I opened my heart to the precious Saviour. Now I am a new man and I live a new life. I am happy in the Lord and I am a blessing to my family." Then he added, "If this Bible is false and if it is a fable and if it is a myth, then what is it that happened to my soul, what happened to my heart, what changed me out of the depths of the mire and set me up before the Lord with my feet on a rock?" The atheist had no answer to that.

This is God's Book and its purpose is salvation. When a man faces despair does he say, "Bring me my book of geology"? When a man faces deep trials of life does he say, "Where is my book of chemistry?" When a man faces the judgment day that is yet to come, does he say, "Where is my book of astronomy?"

When dark days come and we face the swollen river and look over to the other side, how many tears have fallen on the passage in the book of John where the Lord said: "Let not your heart be troubled: ye believe in God, believe also in me. In my Father's house are many mansions. . . . I go to prepare a place for you. And if I go and prepare a place for you, I will come again, and receive you unto myself; that where I am, there ye may be also" (John 14:1-3). And the heart is quieted, and the spirit is comforted, and we have faith and hope and commit ourselves to the love and the grace of God. The Bible is for comfort and assurance of salvation, and that is what it brings to our souls.

Thank God for the Bible,
Whose clear, shining ray
Has lightened our path
And turned night into day.

Its wonderful treasures
Have never been told,
More precious than riches,
Set round with pure gold.

Thank God for the Bible.
In sickness and health,
It brings richer comfort
Than honors or wealth.

Its blessings are boundless,
An infinite store.
We may drink at the fountain,
And thirst nevermore.

Thank God for the Bible.
How dark is the night,
Where no ray from its pages
Sheds forth its pure light.

No Jesus, no Bible,
No heaven of rest,
How could we live,
Were our lives so unblessed?

Thank God for the Bible, the sure, true Word of God. Test it. Try it and know. This is God speaking to our souls.

Chapter 6

Jesus and His Bible

> And beginning at Moses and all the prophets, he expounded unto them in all the scriptures the things concerning himself. . . . And he said unto them, These are the words which I spake unto you, while I was yet with you, that all things must be fulfilled, which were written in the law of Moses, and in the prophets, and in the psalms, concerning me. Then opened he their understanding, that they might understand the scriptures (Luke 24:27, 44, 45).

The Old Testament that I hold in my hand is the Bible that Jesus loved and studied. There are thirty-nine books in the Bible that Jesus loved. There are thirty-nine books in the Old Covenant that I hold in my hand. The words, the books, the Bible that Jesus loved is the Bible that I hold in my hand. Jesus refers to the Scriptures as He knew them in Luke 24:44. From them He showed His disciples what they said about Him (verses 27, 44, 45).

The ancient Jewish people divided the Bible into three parts—the *Torah,* the law of Moses, which we call the Pentateuch; the *Neviim,* the prophets; and the *Kethuvim,* the writings. In theological literature the Kethuvim are called the Hagiographa, the sacred writings. The largest and dominant part of the sacred writings was the Psalms. Jesus called the third division, the *Kethuvim,* the Psalms. In every section of the Scriptures, in every syllable, in every word and in every line, Jesus found Himself. Beginning at Moses and all the prophets (in the *Kethuvim*), He expounded to His disciples the things concerning Himself.

The true modern Jew loves and reverences this Holy Book as did the ancient Jew. Soon after the war between the Arabs and the Jews and the establishment of the Israeli State, I made a visit to Palestine. The one part of the old city that the Jew won for himself and incorporated into Israel is Mount Zion, on which is the tomb of David. At that time, in their love and reverence for that sacred place, the Israeli had a synagogue built over David's tomb. I stayed in that synagogue a long time watching those Jewish refugees and rabbis from the ends of the earth worshiping Jehovah God.

Those old rabbis looked like persons who had stepped out of a picture book with their long, heavy beards, their scull caps, and in some instances (especially among those from Poland), their fur hats with little tassels all around. The rabbis took out of the ark God's scroll. They kissed it as they unclasped it, and as they turned the scroll and read from the sacred page, they kissed the lines on the page. Then having read God's Book, they turned back the scroll and kissed the pages again as they rerolled the manuscript. After that they kissed each one of the clasps, and they kissed the tassels on the scroll. Then they placed it in its case and kissed the case. Finally, they reverently and adoringly placed the scroll back in the ark above the tomb of the great king.

JESUS' REVERENCE FOR THE WORD OF GOD

Jesus reflects in His own life and testimony that holy reverence for the Word of God. How different is our Lord's attitude from the caustic, rationalistic attitude that so many modern theologians assume toward the Holy Word of God. It is a habit, for instance, and has been for generations in circles of pseudo-academic scholastics, to make fun of the story of Jonah. And yet in the twelfth chapter of Matthew, our Lord gives Jonah as a sign and a symbol and a prophecy of the resurrection of His body: "For as Jonas was three days and three nights in the whale's belly; so shall the Son of man be three days and three nights in the heart of the earth" (Matthew 12:40). In the power of God both Jesus and Jonah were raised from the depths of the earth.

In the same false academic circles, it has long been the acceptable theological interpretation that Daniel wrote hundreds of years after the events he describes came to pass, that his prophecy is pseudepigraphous, a false prophecy. But in Matthew 25:15 and the parallel passage in Luke 13:28, our Lord refers to "Daniel, the prophet." To our Lord, the words of Daniel were holy and sacred, harbingers of the coming of the kingdom of God.

Many theological intellectuals look with disdain and scorn upon the book of Genesis. They are evolutionists who reject the narratives of the first book in the Bible. They avow that years ago in their ignorance, gullible people listened to the tales of Genesis as though they were true. But today in our superior intellectual scholasticism we know, these critics say, that there never were such persons as Adam and Eve, there was no such thing as the Garden of Eden, and that all of the rest of those ancient tales are myths and legends. Such is much of modern theology.

But our Lord Jesus looked upon Genesis as one of the great books, holy and divinely inspired, of the sacred Volume. He looked upon Adam and Eve as being real people. In the nineteenth chapter of the book of Matthew He mentioned them as representing God's holy purpose for the human family, that there would be a man for a woman (Matthew 19:3-6).

In the Sermon on the Mount, our Lord declares: "Think not that I am come to destroy the law, or the prophets: I am not come to destroy, but to fulfil." Then He adds: "Till heaven and earth pass, one jot or one tittle shall in no wise pass from the law, till all be fulfilled" (Matthew 5:17, 18). Our Lord is avowing in this remarkable statement that more certain than the continuation of the physical universe is the foundation of the everlasting, unmovable, unchanging Word of God.

That is why when I read the promises in the Old Testament that are yet to be fulfilled, I believe that in God's time and sovereign, elective purpose, they shall yet come to pass.

There is not a jot, there is not a tittle, there is not the dotting of an "i," there is not the crossing of a "t" in the Word of God, but that God shall surely bring it to pass. With regard to the sure continuation of this physical universe, God at one time gave it as a sign of His indestructible, unchanging purpose for His people, Israel.

> Thus saith the Lord, which giveth the sun for a light by day, and the ordinances of the moon and of the stars for a light by night. . . . If those ordinances depart from before me, saith the Lord, then the seed of Israel also shall cease from being a nation before me for ever (Jeremiah 31:35, 36).

"According to the ordinances by which I have ordained the sun and the moon and the stars in heaven," says the Lord God, "by that some sovereignty have I said there shall be an end to my people Israel."

I turn the page and I read in the thirty-second chapter of Jeremiah where the Lord God says:

> I will rejoice over them to do them good, and I will plant them in this land assuredly with my whole heart and with my whole soul. . . . Like as I brought all this evil upon this people [scattered them to the ends of the earth], so will I [bring them back and] bring upon them all the good that I have promised them (Jeremiah 32:41, 42).

Not one jot, not one tittle shall fail in all God's Holy Word.

JESUS LIVED BY THE HOLY SCRIPTURES

Jesus found in that Holy Word the way marked out by which He was to live. "For I say unto you," said our Lord, "that this that is written must yet be accomplished in me" (Luke 22:37). Thinking of His passion, His suffering, agony and death, He quoted the fifty-third chapter of Isaiah, "And he was reckoned among the transgressors." Then He added, "for the things concerning me have an end," that is, they have a fulfillment.

Jesus lived by all of the laws and the prophecies written in the Old Testament; He guided His life by the Word of God. The Word of God in human speech and the life of

God in human flesh are indivisibly, inevitably, eternally and inseparably connected. According to the Scriptures Christ lived. According to the Scriptures Christ died. According to the Scriptures Christ was buried. According to the Scriptures God raised Him from the dead. Jesus not only reflected the old, Jewish reverence and love for the Word of God—He lived it.

Now I shall speak of the way Jesus used the Bible. He used it *for preaching*. In the fourth chapter of Luke we read how the Lord Jesus, after His baptism and temptation, returned in the power of the Spirit to Nazareth where He was brought up, and "as his custom was, he went into the synagogue on the sabbath day, and stood up for to read" (Luke 4:16). (I love that. Jesus "stood up for to read," the Scriptures, just as we do here in this great church.) And they placed in his hand the scroll of the prophet Isaiah. "And when he had opened the book, he found the place where it was written, The Spirit of the Lord is upon me . . . ." Then He quoted the sixty-first chapter of Isaiah, verse 1 and the first part of verse 2: "And he closed the book, and he gave it again to the minister, and sat down. And the eyes of all them that were in the synagogue were fastened on him. And he began to say unto them, This day is this scripture fulfilled in your ears" (verses 17-21).

That is the way Jesus used the Bible. He opened it when He stood up to read, then He delivered His message and His message was an exposition of the Word of God. To you who are in this church that way of expounding God's Word seems quite familiar. It is customary to us. The pastor stands up in the pulpit and opens God's Book and he preaches. But in a multitude of pulpits, for a man to stand up and preach from God's Book is exceptional. There are many, many pulpits where the Bible is hardly referred to; it is never picked up; it is never opened. But when Jesus was in the synagogue "as his custom was," He opened God's Book and He preached to them out of the prophecies of God.

Jesus used His Bible. He used it *for illustrations*. Any

sermon is the richer when the preacher will find the illustrations for his message in the immutable Word of God. So our Lord, in the twelfth chapter of Matthew, used the illustration of the Queen of Sheba who came from afar to see the wisdom and the glory of Solomon. And in Luke 4 from which we have just read, He used the illustration of Elijah and the widow of Sarepta to depict the compassion of God for a poor, Gentile widow (verse 26). In the next verse, He used the story of Elisha and the Syrian leper, Naaman, to illustrate God's compassion for a Syrian soldier.

In talking to Nicodemus (in John 3:14), He illustrated His death, "As Moses lifted up the serpent in the wilderness, even so must the Son of man be lifted up." In talking to the Jews after the feeding of the five thousand (John 6:49), He used the illustration of manna that God sent from heaven to feed His children in the wilderness. And there are many other instances we could give where Jesus used His Bible for illustration.

Jesus also used His Bible *for warning*. In Luke 10:12 He warned the cities inhospitable to His messengers to remember the fate of Sodom when God rained down fire and brimstone from heaven. In that same chapter, He spoke of Tyre and Sidon who would have repented if His great works had been done in their day and in their time (verses 13, 14). Tyre and Sidon will rise in the day of judgment to condemn that generation of Jesus' day. In Luke 17:26-30, He uses illustrations for the coming Judgment Day from the Old Testament: "As it was in the days of Noah, so shall it also be in the days of the Son of man. . . . Likewise also as it was in the days of Lot . . . thus shall it be in the day when the Son of man is revealed." Jesus used His Bible for warning.

Jesus used His Bible as *a weapon* in opposing Satan and in meeting His enemies. Everyone is familiar with the account in the fourth chapter of Matthew of the devil's tempting our Lord in the wilderness: "You are hungry from fasting forty days," said the devil, in effect. "But You are the

Son of God. You have all power. See these stones? Turn them into bread." But God had said that a man was to live by the sweat of his brow. Satan thus sought to undo the incarnation at the very beginning of our Lord's ministry, to entice our Saviour from living the life of a man.

How did our Lord meet the challenge and the trial of Satan? He quoted God's Word from Deuteronomy 8:3: ". . . man doth not live by bread only, but by every word that proceedeth out of the mouth of the Lord doth man live."

In the second temptation, our Lord was taken to the top of the high pinnacle of the temple. "Now, jump down," said Satan, "and let all these people be overwhelmed by the miraculous preservation of your life. Jump and let all the people look on you in awe and in wonder." But the Lord quoted again from Deuteronomy, from chapter 6, verse 16: "Ye shall not tempt the Lord your God."

In the last temptation, on a high mountain, with all the glory of the world passing before the eyes of Jesus, Satan said, "I will give You this if you will fall down and worship me." But Jesus quoted again from the sixth chapter of Deuteronomy, verse 13: "Thou shalt worship the Lord thy God, and him only shalt thou serve." In the trial and battle of life, in the storm and fury of temptation, His weapon in warfare was the Book.

His use of the Scripures in the presence of His enemies is marvelously illustrated in Mark 12:10, 11. Our Lord had just told a parable to those who were seeking to destroy Him—the parable of the vineyard let out to tenants in which the tenants refuse to pay the rent to the owner and kill the owner's servants and finally his son. Continuing His remarks to those who would soon cry "Crucify him! Crucify him!" the Lord said, "Have ye not read this scripture [Psalm 118:22, 23]; The stone which the builders rejected is become the head of the corner: this was the Lord's doing, and it is marvelous in our eyes?" This Jesus that the Jews refused and rejected, this prophet of Nazareth that they condemned and crucified, this Saviour that they nailed to a tree, God has made Him the Lord of the whole creation. It is God's doing and it is marvelous in our eyes.

THE CONVICTING POWER OF THE WORD OF GOD

Now in that same twelfth chapter of Mark we read that the Sadducees came up to Him. They were the rationalists, the secularists of their day — they had all of the answers. They were the materialists—they scoffed at the resurrection, at the idea of heaven, at the idea of a spirit-world. To illustrate their ridicule they told a stock story. For generations they had silenced the Pharisees with that story as they mocked the revelation of God. There was a man who died leaving no children. Following the custom of Levirate marriage, his brother took the wife and sought to raise up children to his dead brother. But this brother died, leaving no children, as did the third brother, the fourth, the fifth, the sixth and the seventh. Finally the woman died. Now in the resurrection, asked the Sadducees as they laughed, whose wife shall she be? All seven had had her.

Thus the Sadducees, who had laughed at the story for generations and had annihilated the Pharisees with it, came to Jesus and told that same old stock tale. But the Lord answered them, "As touching the dead, that they rise: have ye not read in the book of Moses, how in the bush God spake unto him, saying, I am the God of Abraham, and the God of Isaac, and the God of Jacob?" Look closely at these words. The Lord bases His doctrine, His teaching on immortality and the resurrection of the dead on the tense of a verb in the Word of God. "I *am* the God of Abraham, and the God of Isaac, and the God of Jacob. . . . He is not the God of the dead, but the God of the living: ye therefore do greatly err. . . . because ye know not the scriptures, neither the power of God" (Mark 12:26, 27, 24). Isn't that an amazing thing? The whole hope of a resurrection and of a life to come, Jesus bases on the tense of the verb "to be." God never introduced Himself, said Jesus, saying, "I am *going to be* God of my people, or I *was* the God of the dead," but "I *am* the God of the living." If we are God's we live forever.

Again in the same twelfth chapter of Mark, one of the lawyers came and spoke to Jesus. All during their life and their generation, scribes and lawyers had been taking the commandments and measuring them against each other. Some commandments were less and some were greater. Some were lighter and some were heavier. The lawyers' purpose in this was to see how little they could do and still get into the kingdom, and still be saved. They tried to see how little they could give, how little they could love, how little they could serve. They said if you broke a certain commandment it would not matter much, but if you broke certain other ones, it would be a horrendous thing to do.

Some people do the same today. They have venial sins and they have mortal sins. They say you can commit venial sins and get by — they are not fatal. But a mortal sin is deadly. So it was with this rabbinical casuistry. The rabbis took God's commandments and made them great or little in order that they might know which they could break and which they could not break and still be saved. That is what the lawyer had on his mind when he came up to Jesus to entrap Him in His words as he said, "Now which is the great commandment in the Book?" And Jesus never fails to answer. Ask Him and He will have an answer for you. Jesus quoted from the Word of God from Deuteronomy 6:4, 5, the great *Shema*:

> The first of all the commandments is, Hear, O Israel; The Lord our God is one Lord: And thou shalt love the Lord thy God with all thy heart, and with all thy soul, and with all thy mind, and with all thy strength: this is the first commandment. And the second is like unto it [quoting from Leviticus 19:18], namely this, Thou shalt love thy neighbour as thyself. There is none other commandment greater than these.

When the lawyer heard Jesus quote from the Word of God and thus present the great message of time and eternity in the revelation of the Book, he said,

> Master, thou hast said the truth: for there is one God; and there is none other but he: And to love him with all the heart, and with all the understanding, and with all the soul, and with all the strength, and to love his neighbour as himself, is more than all whole burnt offerings and sacrifices.

The Lord, moved by his answer, turned to the lawyer and said, "Thou art not far from the kingdom of God" (Mark 12:29-34).

One is struck by the convicting power of the Word of God when the Lord answered the lawyer, not according to rabbinical casuistry with all of its fine-spun theology in the schools of Hillel and Shammai, but according to the Bible itself. For when the Lord went back to the Book and quoted him the heart of the Bible, that lawyer, immediately moved and convicted, responded: "Master, you have answered right. To love God in a man's soul and to love his neighbor as himself is more than all else." You are near the kingdom when the Word of God enters your heart.

Continuing in this twelfth chapter of Mark, when the scribes, the lawyers, the Sadducees, the Pharisees and the temple authorities and rulers had gathered around Jesus, He proposed asking them a question. He quoted Psalm 110: 1: "David himself said by the Holy Ghost, The Lord [God] said to my Lord [Messiah], Sit thou on my right hand, till I make thine enemies thy footstool. David therefore himself calleth him Lord; and whence is he then his son?"

David said, "The Lord God said to the Messiah [and the Messiah is to be David's son], Lord, sit on my right hand till I annihilate thine enemies." The Lord God called David's son "Lord," and David in the Holy Ghost (see how He makes the Bible the very word of the very breath of God) wrote it down, calling his son, "Lord." But how then is He David's son? Do you look upon your son as Lord? No man ever looked on his son as Lord God, but David did. "How is that?" the Lord asked the Jews. "How do you read? How do you understand the scriptures?"

The next verse says, "And the common people heard him gladly." When Jesus took the Book and opened it and read its pages and quoted its great passages, the common people said: "Amen. Glory to God! Bless the name of the Lord!"

PREACHING FROM THE WORD OF GOD

There is one question asked me more than all others put together. It is known far and wide that I preach the Bible. I have preached through the Bible for many, many years, and the question inevitably asked me is, "Do your people come? Do people come? Do people come just to hear a man preach the Bible?"

They continue by asking, "You are not lecturing on the passing events of the day?" "No," I say, "you can listen to current events on the radio; you can listen to the commentators every hour on the hour and read the editorials in every published newspaper." "Well, what do you do?" they ask. I say, "I just stand up there and open God's Book and say, 'Thus saith the Lord.' " And it is with us as it was in the Bible, "The common people heard him gladly." God's people will always hear God's man gladly when he opens the Book and explains its meaning. Jesus and His Bible!

Jesus *authenticated His ministry* by the Holy Scriptures. Talking to His disciples of the one that would betray Him, He said: "That the scripture may be fulfilled, He that eateth bread with me hath lifted up his heel against me. Now I tell you before it come, that, when it is come to pass, ye may believe that I am he" (John 13:18, 19). He used the Bible to authenticate His mission in the earth as our text says: "And beginning at Moses and all the prophets, he expounded unto them in all the scriptures the things concerning himself." The great witness to the sovereign purpose and will of God in His life was the Scriptures. "This is my Son," this is Jesus, this is Christ the Messiah, the Lord, witnesses the Word of God.

Jesus made the earnest and awesome avowal that if we are to be saved and if we have any hope, it is by listening to the Word of the Lord. In His parable of the rich man and Lazarus, Jesus tells us that Dives prayed, "Send Lazarus to my father's house, for I have five others there, that he may testify unto them lest they come to this awful place of torment. O father Abraham, send Lazarus, raise him from the dead, and let him speak and plead with my five brothers!" Abraham replied, "They have Moses and the prophets. They have the Bible. Let them hear them." And Dives cried, "Father Abraham, No, no; but if one went to them from the dead they would turn, repent." But Abraham said, "If they hear not Moses and the prophets, if they won't listen to the Word of God, neither will they be persuaded though one were raised from the dead."

Lord, open my heart to the message of the Gospel! Lord, open my ears to hear and my eyes to see and my soul to understand, for if I am saved in the judgment that is yet to come, it will be because I listened and opened my heart to the message of the Word of God. God grant that we have embraced the truths of the Bible. Lord Jesus, according to the Holy Word, speak to my soul, bless my life, forgive my sins, stand by me in the Day of Judgment and save me from the wrath to come. And according to Thy Word, bless us, Lord, with Thy favor upon Thy people.

Chapter 7

The Words of This Prophecy

> For I testify unto every man that heareth the words of the prophecy of this book, If any man shall add unto these things, God shall add unto him the plagues that are written in this book: And if any man shall take away from the words of the book of this prophecy, God shall take away his part out of the book of life, and out of the holy city, and from the things which are written in this book (Revelation 22:18, 19).

The Bible closes with words of warning:

> If any man shall add unto these things, God shall add unto him the plagues that are written in this book: And if any man shall take away from the words of the book of this prophecy, God shall take away his part out of the book of life, and out of the holy city, and from the things which are written in this book (Revelation 22:18, 19).

Notice that the inspired apostle does not warn against taking away from the scenes or the imagery or the thoughts of the prophecy. What he wrote was, "If any man shall take away from [the *logia*] the words of the book of this prophecy." The apostle is avowing that in his prophecy are written the veritable words of God.

Now let us understand that we are speaking of the original manuscript, not of its translations. A translation is the result of the finest effort of gifted men to take God's words and put them in another language. Sometimes, of course, men in their human frailties and limitations are not quite able to equate in one language to match the weight of a word in the original language.

In the Amazon jungle last August I was amazed at the

drudgery of one of those translators, toiling over the gospel of Mark, trying to get the gospel of Mark into the language of his jungle tribe. I asked about this tedious toil, his meticulous care. It was taking him years for his work. In defense of his long effort he told of another translator who had not done so well. One of the members of the tribe said to the translator, "You say this is God's Book?" "Yes," said the missionary, "this is God's Book." And the Indian said, "Well, God doesn't speak very good grammar, does He?" That is why this missionary was toiling so to produce a good translation.

THEORIES OF INSPIRATION

I am not speaking of a translation now but of the original manuscripts, the original Word of God. There are several attitudes one can take toward God's Book. You might call them theories of inspiration. Of the many theories, let me briefly name four. First, there are those who look upon God's Book as they would any other piece of antique literature. To them, it is not inspired any more than any other ancient writing is inspired. They look upon it in the same antiquarian way that they would look upon a pot, a piece of pottery, a brick or a weapon dug up from some archaeological survey. They go through a museum where there are artifacts of ancient Persia, of India, of Egypt and of Palestine. Among the bricks and pottery and weapons dug up from an ancient day, they find exhibited some Hebrew manuscripts called "the Bible." To them, there is no more of God in the Bible than there is in the Egyptian Book of the Dead or the Rig-Veda of India.

Then there is a second attitude toward the Word of God. There are those who believe that it is a product of man's intuition. The fact that we are capable of discernment, that we have intuitive faculties and understanding, applies to all of human accomplishment. In the world of materialism, our intuitive faculties bring to us all the marvels of science. By our mind's eye, we are able to see these marvels and to pluck such things as the radio waves out of what cannot be seen and use them for scientific purposes. Applied to knowledge, intuition gives birth to philosophy or beautiful literature or operas or other things that we enjoy. Applied to painting, it gives birth to art. According to that school of thought, man's intuitive faculties applied to the spiritual world gave birth to the Word of God. They believe the Scriptures are no more inspired than a man is inspired who would paint a beautiful painting or write a beautiful song or discover some great fact in the scientific world. The Bible, they say, is just a product of man's genius, of his own power to create.

A third attitude toward the Word of God is one of spiritual illumination. Every child of God, these men would say, has an inner illumination. The men who wrote the Bible had that illumination to a greater degree than do the rest of us, being more spiritually sensitive. God has not revealed objective truths, according to this view. All that is written in the Word of God is subjective; man's spiritual sensitivity has given birth to this Book.

Then there are those who believe as I do, that the Word of the Bible is inspired—a plenary, verbal inspiration. The Bible does not *contain* God's Word; it *is* God's Word. This is what God has said, and when I read this Holy Book I am reading God's words; I am following God's language and thinking God's thoughts. Did God say anything? Does God speak? My heart answers "Yes." God speaks and what God says I can read in the holy, sacred and inviolable volume that I hold in my hand. This sermon is a presentation of my belief and persuasion that this Bible is verbally, plenarily inspired.

When I turn to the Book itself, I am amazed and overwhelmed by the claims of those who wrote it. In the thirty-nine books of the Old Testament, the phrase "Thus saith the Lord" is repeated more than two thousand, six hundred times. More than 2600 times in the thirty-nine books of the Old Testament we read that "God said this"! The writers were claiming that God speaks to man and that the words they wrote are the words of God.

In preparing this sermon, I read of a man who said that if the men who wrote over two thousand six hundred times that God spoke to them, claiming that they were inspired of God to write what they did, were not writing by inspiration, these authors were the most compulsive and confirmed liars and deceivers that the world has ever seen. Then he added, "Can you imagine a group of men over a period of years telling over two thousand six hundred lies about the same thing? That ought to be a record that should stand!" I agree with him. The writers of the Bible make a definite avowal that they are writing the words of God; they avow it again and again; they affirm it and re-affirm it.

I have chosen just one page of the Bible which is typical of all the pages. Notice I will not turn a leaf. Observe how many times, as I read from this one page, the holy prophet of God will avow and confirm that the words he delivers are the words of the unchanging God. I read:

> The words of Jeremiah the son of Hilkiah . . . to whom the words of the Lord came in the days of Josiah the son of Amon king of Judah . . . . also in the days of Jehoiakim the son of Josiah king of Judah . . . . Then the word of the Lord came unto me, saying . . . . But the Lord said unto me . . . . Be not afraid of their faces: for I am with thee . . . . Then the Lord put forth his hand, and touched my mouth. And the Lord said unto me, Behold I have put my words in thy mouth. . . . Moreover the word of the Lord came unto me, saying . . . . Then said the Lord unto me . . . . And the word of the Lord came unto me the second time . . . . Then the Lord said unto me . . . . for I am with thee, saith the Lord, to deliver thee. Moreover the word of the Lord came to me, saying, Go and cry in the ears of Jerusalem, saying, Thus saith the Lord . . . . Thus saith the Lord (Jeremiah 1:1-19; 2:1-5).

This leaf is typical of the whole Word of God. These men who gave the Word of God, apostles, prophets, ambassadors from the courts of heaven, with illimitable, unfathomable, and immeasurable assurance, avowed that the word they delivered was the Word of the Living God.

DIFFERENT WAYS GOD SPOKE IN THE BIBLE

I want you to notice how often it is said that God spoke in an audible voice, that God used words and language. In the very beginning, when Adam and Eve disobeyed God's command and hid themselves, what does the Word say? "And they heard the voice of the Lord God walking in the garden in the cool of the day" (Genesis 3:8). They heard the voice. They had been accustomed to talking with God and they recognized the voice of the Almighty, for God uses words. "And the Lord God called unto Adam, and said unto him, Where art thou?" (verse 9). Adam heard the voice and understood the words of God.

Here are just a few examples of the words used by God, examples which are typical of many such instances. Moses, on the backside of the desert, saw a bush burning unconsumed. The Lord God spoke to Moses out of the burning bush, "Moses, Moses." And Moses replied, "Here am I." And the Lord God said, "Put off thy shoes from off thy feet, for the place whereon thou standest is holy ground. Moreover he said, I am the God of Abraham, the God of Isaac, and the God of Jacob" (Exodus 3:1-6). God was speaking audibly. God uses words.

When we come to the record of the birth of the Mosaic legislation, how awe-inspiring is the voice of God:

> And mount Sinai was altogether on a smoke, because the Lord descended upon it in fire: and the smoke thereof ascended as the smoke of a furnace, and the whole mount quaked greatly. And when the voice of the trumpet sounded long, and waxed louder and louder, Moses spake, and God answered him by a voice (Exodus 19:18).
>
> And all the people saw the thunderings, and the lightnings, and the noise of the trumpet, and the mountain smoking: and when the people saw it, they removed, and stood afar off. And they said unto Moses, Speak thou with us, and we will hear: but let not God speak with us, lest we die" (Exodus 20:18, 19).

So awesome and so terrible was the voice of the living God that the people said, "You tell us, Moses, what God says. Let not God speak to us face to face lest we die."

After the Law was given and the Tabernacle erected, we read:

> And when Moses was gone into the tabernacle of the congregation to speak with him, then he heard the voice of one speaking unto him from off the mercy seat that was upon the ark of testimony, from between the two cherubims: and he spake unto him (Numbers 7:89).

God spoke to Moses. "The Lord spake unto Moses face to face, as a man speaketh unto his friend" (Exodus 33:11).

In the night time when the child Samuel lay asleep in the tabernacle, old Eli was the pastor presiding over the house of God at Shiloh. And the voice of God spoke to Samuel saying, "Samuel, Samuel." The little boy did not know that God spoke. So he ran to old Eli and said, "Here am I, for thou didst call me." Eli said: "I did not call thee. Lie down again." And the second time God called Samuel, saying, "Samuel, Samuel." And the second time Samuel went to Eli. The third time that God said, "Samuel, Samuel," and the little boy ran to Eli, the old priest realized that God was speaking to the child. Old Eli then said to the little boy, "Son, the next time you hear the voice, answer, 'Speak, Lord, for thy servant heareth.'" And the Lord spoke in an audible voice a prophecy to the child Samuel.

Let us turn to the Book and see how God's words were recorded. One time they were written by God Himself. At the end of the thirty-first chapter of Exodus, we read that God gave to Moses, "when he had made an end of communing with him upon mount Sinai, two tables of testimony, tables of stone, written with the finger of God" (Exodus 31:18). These are words of God recorded on tables of stone, written by the finger of God. In the same way, that hand wrote on the wall at Belshazzar's feast, "Mene, Mene, Tekel, Upharsin" (Daniel 5:25).

In this Holy Book, it is avowed again and again that inspired prophets and apostles wrote down God's words. For instance, in Exodus 20:1 we read, "And God spake all these words, saying . . . ." Then I turn to chapter 24, verse 4: "And Moses wrote all the words of the Lord." In that same chapter, verse 12: "And the Lord said unto Moses, Come up to me into the mount, . . . and I will give thee tables of stone, and a law, and commandments which I have written; that thou mayest teach them." After the voice and the revelation, and after the speech of God, Moses wrote down the words of Almighty God (see Exodus 34:28). Such statements are repeated throughout the whole Bible.

In the twenty-third chapter of II Samuel, David is described as speaking from his death-bed:

> Now these be the last words of David. David the son of Jesse said, and the man who was raised up on high, the anointed of the God of Jacob, and the sweet psalmist of Israel, said, The Spirit of the Lord spake by me, and his word was in my tongue. The God of Israel said, the Rock of Israel spake to me (verses 1 and 2).

David wrote down what the Rock of Israel, what the God of Israel said to him.

Let us read one other passage in the thirty-sixth chapter of the prophet Jeremiah:

> And it came to pass in the fourth year of Jehoiakim the son of Josiah king of Judah, that this word came unto Jeremiah from the Lord, saying, Take thee a roll of a book [a scroll], and write therein all the words that I have spoken unto thee. . . . Then Jeremiah called Baruch the son of Neriah: and Baruch wrote from the mouth of Jeremiah all the words of the Lord, which he had spoken unto him, upon a roll of a book (Jeremiah 36:1, 2, 4).

These are God's words, and Jeremiah dictated them to Baruch as God spoke them to him.

The rest of the story in the thirty-sixth chapter of Jeremiah is that when Jehoiakim the king heard that the scroll was written, he sent Jehudi to fetch the roll and to read it to him.

> Jehudi [stood before the king and] read it in the ears of the king . . . . Now the king sat in the winterhouse . . . and there was a fire on the hearth burning before him. And it came to pass, that when Jehudi had read three or four leaves [had turned the scroll three or four times], he cut it with the penknife, and cast it into the fire . . . until all the roll was consumed in the fire that was on the hearth (Jeremiah 36:20-23).

But can you burn up God's Book? Can you destroy God's revelation? Can you?

> Then the word of the Lord came to Jeremiah, after that the king had burned the roll . . . saying, Take thee again another roll, and write in it all the former words that were in the first roll, which Jehoiakim the king of Judah hath burned (Jeremiah 36:27, 28).

God's Word is indestructible, imperishable. God's Word is like Himself, the same yesterday and today and forever. Our Lord said that when this heaven and this earth have passed away, God's Word shall endure immovable, unchangeable forever.

THE NEW TESTAMENT TESTIFIES TO THE WORDS OF GOD

Turning to the New Testament one finds that the apostles looked upon the words written in the Old Testament as being the words of God. Matthew records his view in this way. The angel of the Lord said to Joseph,

> She shall bring forth a son, and thou shalt call his name JESUS: for he shall save his people from their sins. Now all this was done that it might be fulfilled which was spoken of the Lord by the prophet, saying, Behold, a virgin shall be with child, and shall bring forth a son, and they shall call his name Emmanuel . . . God with us (Matthew 1:21-23).

After the birth of Jesus, Mary and Joseph fled into Egypt. Matthew records that they were there "until the death of Herod: that it might be fulfilled which was spoken of the Lord by the prophet, saying, Out of Egypt have I called my son" (Matthew 2:14, 15). The attitude, holy and reverential, of the apostles and the authors of the New Testament is that when they read the Old Testament Scriptures they were reading the words of God.

Now I shall sum up briefly what could be spoken of at great length concerning the inspiration of the Holy Scriptures in the New Covenant, the New Testament. In the fourteenth chapter of the gospel of John, the Lord said: "But the Comforter [the *Paraclete*], which is the Holy Ghost, whom the Father will send in my name, he shall teach you all things, and bring all things to your remembrance, whatsoever I have said unto you" (John 14:26). Later in that last talk with His disciples, Jesus told them that "when he, the Spirit of truth, is come, he will guide you into all truth: for he shall not speak of himself; but whatsoever he shall hear, that shall he speak: and he will shew you things to come. He shall glorify me: for he shall receive of mine, and shall shew it unto you" (John 16:13, 14).

Here, first, is the pre-authentication of the inspiration of the New Testament. What was written and what those apostles delivered was what the Holy Spirit placed in their hearts, brought to their remembrance and confirmed as being the true revelation from God.

Second, here is assurance and a guarantee of the inerrancy, the absolute accuracy of what is written in these New Testament pages. This is what God, by the Holy Spirit, wanted the apostles to write down. For example, the Apostle Paul wrote to the Galatians: "I certify you, brethren, that the gospel which was preached of me is not after man. For I neither received it of man, neither was I taught it, but by the revelation of Jesus Christ" (Galatians 1:11). The words that he spoke and the Gospel that he delivered was one that God, by revelation, placed in his soul and on his lips.

Every time we have the Lord's Supper I read the passage: "For I have received of the Lord that which also I delivered unto you" (I Corinthians 11:23). God said it to Paul, and

Paul wrote it down in the Book. You notice the same source of inspiration in the life and writings of the Apostle Peter. He wrote to his readers, "That ye may be mindful of the words which were spoken before by the holy prophets, and of the commandment of us the apostles of the Lord and Saviour" (II Peter 3:2). The words that are spoken by the prophets and the apostles are the words of God.

The glorious unfolding of the times yet to come that was given to the sainted Apostle John on the Isle of Patmos came from God. John writes:

> I John, who also am your brother and companion in tribulation and in the kingdom and patience of Jesus Christ, was in the isle that is called Patmos. . . . I was in the Spirit on the Lord's day, and heard behind me a great voice, as of a trumpet, saying, I am Alpha and Omega, the first and the last: and, What thou seest, write in a book, and send it unto the seven churches which are in Asia (Revelation 1:9-11).

John wrote down, according to the voice that spoke to him, the words and the revelation of Almighty God.

In the thirty-seventh chapter of Jeremiah, King Zedekiah asked the prophet: "Is there any word from the Lord?" (Jeremiah 37:17). Does God speak? Does God say anything? The cry of science through the voice of one of its greatest exponents and proponents said, "The silence of the universe frightens me." Men can find no answer in science. Likewise men can hear no voice from the grave. As they can hear no voice from the spheres so they can hear no voice from the dead. There is no voice heard in the universe around us, nor is there a prospective, answering hope in the unfolding of the ages to come or in the discoveries of science. Their prophets are seers of despair and sterility and darkness and death.

The cry of the modern age is like the cry of King Zedekiah, "O, Jeremiah, prophet of God, is there any word from the Lord?" Does God speak? Has God said anything? In this vale of tears, in this long, long journey that all of us inevitably take, is there any meaning? Is there any hope for us? Is there any destiny before us? Does God say anything? "Jeremiah, is there any word from the Lord?" Jeremiah replies: "There is," and proceeds to deliver to the king the prophecy of the great sovereign God of time and destiny and history.

We bring our humbled, baffled souls to Jesus today. Lord, is there any word? Does God speak? We turn to the holy Book and there we find the plenitude of God's loving and merciful care for His own. Our Lord said, "Man shall not live by bread alone, but by every word that proceedeth out of the mouth of God" (Matthew 4:4). We possess God's word in the Bible. We hear God's voice in the Holy Scriptures.

Thou truest friend man ever knew,
Thy constancy I've tried;
When all were false, I found thee true,
My counselor and guide.

The mines of earth no treasures give,
That could this volume buy,
In teaching me the way to live,
It taught me how to die.

"The grass withereth, the flower fadeth: but the word of our God shall abide for ever" (Isaiah 40:8) — blessed, precious, unchanging Saviour revealed to us in the pages of the Holy Scriptures.

Chapter 8

The War Over the Word

> Take heed therefore unto yourselves, and to all the flock, over the which the Holy Ghost hath made you overseers, to feed the church of God, which he hath purchased with his own blood. For I know this, that after my departing shall grievous wolves enter in among you, not sparing the flock. Also of your own selves shall men arise, speaking perverse things, to draw away disciples after them (Acts 20:28-30).

This message could well be entitled *The Destruction of the Christian Faith.* It could well be entitled *The Destruction of Our Hope in God.* We could entitle it *The Destruction of the City Church,* because I think in terms of my ministry here in this pulpit. I am taking a city church as an example of how the faith, the foundation, the very existence of the witness for Christ in His Church can be destroyed.

In Acts 20 Paul is talking to the elders of the Ephesian church, and he says to them in the twenty-eighth verse:

> Take heed therefore unto yourselves . . . to feed the church of God. . . . For I know . . . that after my departing shall grievous wolves enter in among you, not sparing the flock. Also of your own selves shall men arise, speaking perverse things, to draw away disciples after them.

That was the prophecy that the apostle made concerning the church in the city of Ephesus.

In a letter that Paul wrote to Timothy, his son in the ministry and the pastor of the church at Ephesus, he defines a part of that attack thus:

> . . . in the last days perilous times shall come. . . . Evil men and seducers [a better translation would be *imposters*] shall

> wax worse and worse, deceiving and being deceived. But continue thou in the things which thou hast learned and hast been assured of, knowing . . . that from a child thou hast known the holy scriptures, which are able to make thee wise unto salvation. . . . All scripture is given by inspiration of God [not a part of Scripture, not a piece of it, not a fragment of it, but from the first letter in Genesis to the last benedictory *amen* in the Revelation] (II Timothy 3:1, 13-16).

In the same breath that Paul spoke of imposters and evil men and deceivers, he made appeal to the pastor of the church, his son in the ministry, to be true to the Scriptures, saying, "All scripture is given by inspiration of God [*theopneustos*]." It is God-breathed.

The tragic prophecy of Paul sorrowfully came to pass. As the days multiplied and the years followed one after another, to this same church at Ephesus the Lord addressed a letter through John in the Revelation: "I have somewhat against thee, because thou hast left thy first love" (Revelation 2:4). The imposter, the deceiver, the pseudo-superior theologian who presented himself as having a greater *gnosis*, a higher knowledge, did his evil work effectively. The church lost its love for the message of the Book. The foundation of their hope and their faith had been undermined, eaten away, destroyed.

The Christian faith cannot continue in power, a church cannot increase as a burning and a shining light for Christ, when the persuasion of its pastor, of its leaders, of its membership is that the message of the Bible is just another piece of literature out of the ancient past. For when we lose our persuasion and our conviction that this is the unchanging revelation of God, written by God Himself through human hands, we lose all of the basis for our faith in God and our salvation in Jesus Christ.

THE LION'S ATTACK ON DANIEL

Out of the many focal points of the assault of modern destructive criticism, I have chosen to discuss the Book of Daniel. I could have chosen the Virgin Birth. Modern liberalism is almost unanimous in its rejection of the Virgin Birth. But having spoken upon it several times, I have chosen to discuss another section of the Bible which also bears the brunt of modern pseudo-intellectualism—the Book of Daniel. With unbelievable unanimity, the whole pseudo-intellectual modernistic world repudiates the Book of Daniel. That sort of attack goes back just about as far into the dim past as the story of the Christian message itself. For Satan is clever enough to know that if he can destroy the Bible, if he can destroy men's confidence in the authority of the Word of God, then it is axiomatic that faith itself will disintegrate.

In A.D. 275, Porphyry, a brilliant Neo-Platonist philosopher of Alexandria, avowed in his bitter attack against the Christian faith that there is no such thing as prophecy, that men cannot foretell coming events. He took as the focal point of his assault the prophecy of Daniel. This bitter heathen who assailed the Christian faith said that the Book of Daniel was a fraud and a forgery written about 150 to 100 B.C., in the days of the Maccabees. He said it falsely claimed to have been written about 550 B.C. He said that all of the prophecies of Daniel were written after the events had come to pass; and that in order to make it look like prophecy, Daniel, or whoever was called Daniel, made as though the volume had been written in the sixth century B.C. Porphyry claimed that by 150 B.C. all that Daniel, whoever he was, had written was already history, and Daniel made it look as though he were writing prophecy.

So Porphyry labeled Daniel a fraud and a forgery. That verdict has become the universal verdict of the modernist and the liberal to this present hour. To him there is no such thing as the supernatural; there is no such thing as the intervention of God in human history; there is no such thing as prediction; there is no such thing as prophecy; there is no such thing as a man's being able to foretell coming events. Therefore Daniel is a fraud and a forgery.

Now, let's study the matter in the light of the past and

of the present day. The liberal, the pseudo-intellectual, the modern destructive critic, has said Daniel was certainly written in 150 B.C. in the days of the Maccabees. Let us face his accusation frankly, honestly and openly. First of all, turning to the Word of God, in Matthew 24:15, I read from the great apocalyptic discourse of our Saviour this word: "When ye therefore shall see the abomination of desolation, spoken of by Daniel the prophet, stand in the holy place, (whoso readeth, let him understand)." The fact to be emphasized here is this: Jesus did not consider Daniel a deceiver or a forger. Our Saviour called Daniel "the prophet."

THE SEPTUAGINT TRANSLATION AND THE BOOK OF DANIEL

In the second place, consider the most famous of all the translations of the Scriptures ever made, the Septuagint, the ancient Greek translation of the Hebrew Old Testament Scriptures. This is the Bible that the apostles held in their hands when they preached the Gospel of the Son of God. They preached in a Greek-speaking world. When Paul wrote to Latin Rome, he wrote his epistle in Greek. Wherever literate men lived in the Roman Empire, they spoke Greek, so naturally the New Testament was written in the universal language, Greek. The Greek translation of the Old Testament called "The Seventy," the Septuagint (after the seventy men who worked on it), was made beginning under the Ptolemies in Alexandria about 300 B.C.

When I turn, therefore, to the Septuagint, I find Genesis. So that book was certainly written by the time of the translation. Then I turn the pages and here are Exodus, Leviticus, Numbers, Deuteronomy, and every one of the books of the Old Testament — including Daniel. Yet the critics say that Daniel was not written until 150 B.C.! Here in the Bible that the apostles used when they preached the Gospel of Jesus, in the translation of the Old Testament Scriptures made about 300 B.C., is the Book of Daniel.

A gifted professor who loves God and loves the Word is a faithful member of our church. He is professor of Hebrew in Southwestern Baptist Theological Seminary. He is also interested in archaeology. A few weeks ago there was a splendid article in our daily newspapers about some of the archaeological discoveries that he has made in the vicinity of Hebron. Not far from where this scholar in archaeology is probing into the cultures of the past is Qumran, on the western side of the Dead Sea. The hills here are filled with caves. Inside a number of the caves archaeologists have discovered scrolls and fragments of practically every Old Testament book. They were copied about 150 B.C. and after, in the days of the Maccabees. Thus they are 900 or 1,000 years older than any other Hebrew Old Testament manuscript we have which contains the Masoretic text on which our present translations of the Old Testament are based.

Among the scrolls discovered at Qumran are fragments of the Book of Daniel. This means that at the very time the forgery Daniel was being composed, according to critics, it already existed as a part of the Old Testament and was being copied.

I am reminded of the critics who were tearing up the gospel of John, saying that no such gospel could have been written by the apostle so soon after the death of Christ because it would have taken years and centuries for such a gospel message to be developed. So they said that John was not written until at least 250 years after Christ. And while the critical theological world was saying that, there was discovered in the sands of Egypt a scrap of papyrus which was part of a collection of Biblical books and was written about A.D. 90 to 95. On it are portions of the gospel of John! Does that convince the critics? No! Nor are they convinced about the authorship of Daniel. They still insist that God cannot intervene in history, that there is no such thing as the supernatural, that there are no such things as miracles, that there is no such thing as prophecy or predicting the events of the future. To them, therefore, Daniel no matter what is a forgery and a fraud.

Whoever wrote the Book of Daniel was a tremendous

man and a great prophet. Yet he is entirely unknown in the days when the critics say he lived. How amazing! The books I and II Maccabees, written around that time, have come down to us. You will find them in the Apocrypha. Over and over, time and again in those books is the lament that there is no prophet, there is no man of God. From Malachi, in 400 B.C., to John the Baptist, A.D. 30, there were no prophets. We can well understand, then, the lament in the Book of the Maccabees. Yet that is the time when the critics say Daniel lived and wrote his prophecy.

In the Book of Ezekiel, however, you will find several places where Ezekiel honors Daniel, his older contemporary, as a great prophet and holy man of God. Yet the critics say that Daniel is a fraud and a forgery and that it was composed in 150 B.C.

JOSEPHUS AND THE BOOK OF DANIEL

Let us look now at the testimony of Josephus. Josephus was the famous Jewish historian who lived in the first century A.D., a contemporary of Paul and John. He took the name *Flavius Josephus* because he was befriended by the Flavian Emperors Vespasian and his two sons, Titus and Domitian. Josephus was a general in the war of rebellion against Rome that ended in the destruction of the nation in A.D. 70. He headed the army of Galilee. When he was defeated, he remained with Vespasian and later with Titus, pleading with his Jewish countrymen to lay down their arms of insurrection. For his friendship and for his ability to write, he was much honored by the Roman Caesars of the Flavian house. His history of the Jews is one of the greatest pieces of historical narrative to be found in all literature.

In the volume *Antiquities of the Jews*, we find Josephus' record of the conquering of the civilized world by Alexander the Great. In Book XI, chapter 8 and paragraphs 3, 4 and 5, Josephus says that at this time (332 B.C.), Alexander crossed over the Hellespont, fought the great battle against the Persians at Isis in Silicia (in the corner of the Mediterranean where it ceases going eastward and turns down straight south) and overwhelming the armies of Persia, came into Syria and took Damascus. Then he conquered Sidon. Then he besieged Tyre. Nebuchadnezzar had besieged Tyre for months and years and never was able to capture the fortress. The only time in the history of the world that Tyre was ever captured was when Alexander the Great did it in 332 B.C.

While Alexander the Great was besieging Tyre, Josephus says, he sent word to Jaddua, the High Priest at Jerusalem who ruled over Judea, that the Jews send him provisions, send him food and help in his siege against the city. Jaddua, the High Priest, answered Alexander and said that he had sworn by an oath to be true to Darius and he could not break that oath. Upon receiving this answer, Alexander was very angry, and after he had reduced Tyre, he said, "I am going up to that city of Jerusalem and waste it and slay that high priest for not helping me in my hour of great need."

After Alexander the Great (I am just summarizing the story in the history of Josephus) had reduced Tyre and for the first time in history had taken that bastion, he went down and conquered Egypt, then Gaza. After he had taken Gaza, he hurried up to Jerusalem. When Jaddua, the High Priest, heard that Alexander was coming, he was in terror, not knowing how he should meet the Macedonian, since the king was displeased because he had refused to give him food for his soldiers against Tyre. Then it was, Josephus says, that Jaddua took the matter to God in prayer and asked all the people to make supplication to Jehovah. God told him in a dream that he was to take courage and adorn the city and open the gates, and that all the priests should appear in white garments and go out to meet Alexander in the habits of their order, without dread of ill consequences.

Alexander came up from Gaza to destroy Jerusalem, accompanied by a horde of people from all over the world who followed him to pillage the holy city, to sell the people into slavery, and to watch him put the High Priest to death. But when he arrived with his army to destroy Jerusalem, he saw that holy band of God's people pouring out of the city. The city was adorned, the gates opened and there came the High Priest, dressed in his garments of beauty. He was attired in purple and in scarlet, with the mitre upon his head, and the beautiful robes flowing from his shoulders and waist. On his breast was the golden plate with the twelve precious stones, whereon is inscribed the name of the Lord God. When Alexander the Great met the resplendent High Priest coming out of the city of Jerusalem, he fell down in his presence and called on the name of God Jehovah.

One of the leaders of the army came up to Alexander after this amazing act of humble obeisance, and said, "Why are you bowing, you, who never bowed before any man, you, who conquered the world? Why are you worshiping before this High Priest?" And Alexander the Great replied: "I did not adore him, but that God who hath honored him with his high priesthood; for I saw this very person in a dream, in this very habit, in this very dress, when I was at Dios in Macedonia, who, when I was considering how I might conquer Asia, informed me to make no delay but to cross the Hellespont with my army." Then Alexander the Great accompanied the High Priest and the people of Jerusalem into the holy city; and when he went up into the Temple, he offered sacrifices to Jehovah God.

It was at this triumphant moment that the Book of Daniel was shown to him. (Remember, this is 330 B.C., and yet the entire liberal world says the book was not written until 150 B.C.!) I am reading from Josephus: "And when the Book of Daniel was showed him, wherein Daniel declared that one of the Greeks should destroy the Empire of the Persians . . . he was glad. . . ." Thus Josephus describes the dramatic story.

Where in Daniel could the High Priest show Alexander

the Great the prophecy of his coming? In the eighth chapter, the prophet describes the conquest of the Persians. Then he proceeds to describe the destruction of the Persian Empire by a great king of the Greeks. In verses 20, 21 and following, he identifies the kingdoms and the king. No wonder Alexander was impressed. No wonder! Any fair-minded man would be impressed.

PROPHECIES OF DANIEL FULFILLED TODAY

But we need not turn back to Josephus for confirmation of Daniel as a prophet. We need not turn back to the Septuagint. We need not turn back to these ancient histories that confirm the fulfillment of the prophecies of Daniel. Let us look about us today. We can test the book, measure it, place a canon by the side of it today. For Daniel's prophecies reach to the consummation of the age, to the end-time. Are they being fulfilled? Are they true? Are they from God? Let us read and see.

Daniel saw as a revelation from God a portrayal of all history of mankind from his day to the Second Coming of Christ. The youth Daniel was taken captive in 605 B.C. by the armies of Babylon under Nebuchadnezzar. His prophecy begins with that first kingdom. In the vision given to Nebuchadnezzar, the king saw a great image in the form of a man with a head of gold. God told Daniel that the head of gold represented the Babylonian kingdom, the beginning of the times of the Gentiles. Then the breast and arms were of silver, signifying the dual kingdom of Medo-Persia. The thighs were of brass, representing the great kingdom of the Greeks. The two legs of the image were made of iron, the strongest of all. They symbolize the eastern and the western parts of the Roman Empire. The feet and the toes of the image were made out of iron and clay. This, God told Daniel, meant there would never be another universal kingdom. There would never be another world empire. But there would be many nations, some weak, some strong, some iron, some clay.

Have these things come to pass? Was the Babylonian kingdom succeeded by the Medo-Persian? Was the Medo-Persian kingdom succeeded by the Greek? Was the Greek kingdom succeeded by the Roman Empire? And is it true that there never has been a world kingdom, a world empire, since the days of the fall of the Roman Empire? You can see today that some nations are weak and some are strong, but there has not been (and never will be until the consummation) since the end of the Roman Empire a universal kingdom in this world. That is what Daniel says. Is that the way it is coming out? Is that the way history is being made today? Precisely.

Again in the ninth chapter, Daniel made a prophecy by the Spirit of God, saying that unto the end, wars and desolations are determined. Is that true? Let us see. In February 1914 there were gathered in Los Angeles, California, in a prophetic conference, some godly men who loved the Holy Scriptures. The members of the conference gave special attention to those prophecies of the Lord and of the Holy Word that nation should rise against nation and kingdom against kingdom, and that these terrible wars would be followed by famines and inevitable pestilence.

When the liberal world heard of that prophetic conference, one of them, the editor of the *Christian Advocate*, called it a "pathetic conference" — not a *prophetic* conference but a *pathetic* conference. For, said these dreamers of the golden age created by the ingenuity of man, wars are to be no more. We are beating our spears into plowshares; we are learning war no more. At the persuasion of these empty dreamers, America was throwing away her blueprints of dreadnoughts and battleships because we were forever thereafter to live in a world of peace, wrought by legislation and culture and all of the accouterments of higher learning. That was in February, 1914, when the intellectual and the liberal made fun of the "pathetic conference" in Los Angeles.

But what happened? Within a few months, the Archduke

of Austria was slain by an assassin in Serbia and the whole civilized world was plunged into the dreadful holocaust of the first World War. After that war was over, Germany lived for nothing else but the day when she could avenge her blood and her destruction. And we faced World War II, and after World War II, the Korean War. And after Korea it is Red China and Viet-Nam. Isn't this a strange thing? We are not at war, but American boys are dying every day in a battle that never ceases in that little peninsula of southeast Asia. You see, Daniel said wars are determined to the end. It is difficult for even the pseudo-intellectual ultimately to deny the truth of the living God.

As long as we hold to our hearts this Holy Book, with its revelation from the God of heaven who can see the end from the beginning, we have a message that can save our souls. Its precepts are the great foundations upon which human lives and homes are built. As long as the Bible is the course of our doctrine and of our preaching; as long as its message is our faith; as long as God's Word is dear to us — the Word Incarnate which is Jesus, the Word written which is the Holy Bible, the Word spoken by the mouth of the living God which the prophets and apostles heard — as long as the Word is precious to our souls, we have hope, we have faith, we have strength, we have salvation, we have heaven and all that God has prepared for those who love Him. But when the basis of our persuasion and of our hope is destroyed, the whole revelation of God in Christ turns to dust and ashes in our hands. There is then no authority, no revelation, no ultimate Word, and we live in a world of hopeless and darkening despair. Blessed Book!

> The mines of earth no treasures give,
> That could the volume buy;
> In teaching me the way to live
> It taught me how to die.
>
> — GEORGE POPE MORRIS

Chapter 9

The Preservation of the Word of God

> The grass withereth, the flower fadeth: but the word of our God shall stand for ever ((Isaiah 40:8).

This message is built around three passages and three words. One is in the Psalms, a Hebrew word in a Hebrew verse. The second is in I Peter 1, a Greek word in a Greek verse. The third is in the fortieth chapter of Isaiah, a Hebrew word in a Hebrew verse.

We turn first to Psalm 119:89. The 119th Psalm is by far the longest chapter in the Bible. It has one hundred seventy-six verses and every one but six of those verses mentions the Word of God. It is a paean of praise, thanksgiving and adoration to God for His immutable, unchanging Word. Verse 89 reads, "For ever, O Lord, thy word *natsab* in heaven." In the King James Version it reads, "For ever, O Lord, thy word is settled in heaven." That is a good translation of *natsab*. "For ever, O Lord, thy word is *fixed* in heaven, thy word is *established* in heaven, thy word is settled in heaven." What the divinely inspired Psalmist is saying is that before the Word was delivered on earth, the Word existed in heaven. This Book written on earth is but a copy of what God has written in heaven.

The whole Psalm is written in that tenor. For example, verse 152: "Concerning thy testimonies . . . thou hast founded them for ever"; verse 160: "Thy word is true from the beginning . . . endureth for ever"; and our text, "For ever, O Lord, thy word is settled in heaven." These Holy

Scriptures are but a copy of what God has written and fixed forever in heaven.

GOD'S WORD THE SAME FOREVER

Washington, D.C., is the home of the Bureau of Standards. Every weight and every measure that is used in the United States is a copy of the standard that is kept inviolate by the Bureau in Washington. In that Bureau there is a perfect inch, a perfect foot, a perfect yard, a perfect gallon, a perfect pint, a perfect millimeter, a perfect milligram. Every weight and measure that we have finds its standard in that Bureau in Washington, and all are judged by that standard. They follow the rule held inviolate in Washington.

In the Naval Observatory in Washington, there is a chronometer that is corrected by astonomical observation every day at 12:00 o'clock noon. Time in America is kept correct by checking with those astronomical observations every day at high noon. Then that time is communicated to all of the clocks and timepieces in the United States. The time on the dials of the clocks all over America is a repercussion, a copy of the paragon of excellence and perfection in that Naval Observatory in Washington, D.C.

So the Psalmist says that this Word that we hold in our hands is but a copy of that perfect and fixed and unchanging Word of God in heaven. It was there in the beginning. It shall be there world without end, kept inviolate and inerrant by the sovereign God. Thousands of years ago there were thirty-nine books in the Old Testament. Today there are thirty-nine books in the Old Testament. In the first Christian century there were twenty-seven books in the New Testament. Today there are twenty-seven books in the New Testament. This Book is kept inviolate and inerrant by the Word of God, by the power of the Lord, by the mandates of the Almighty. Every jot and every tittle has been kept just as it was through the thousands of years. They have never been changed.

Take a look sometime at a Hebrew Bible. It starts at the

back and goes to the front. A page starts at the right side and reads to the left side. When you go to the Jewish people and ask why they do all this reading backward, they answer, "Who was doing it first?"! The Hebrew words go along, page after page, one column to a page. Then suddenly, for no reason at all, the pages are divided into separated columns, a form the Jews call "brick-work." And every Hebrew Bible in the whole, wide world for thousands of years, ever since there has been a Hebrew Bible, follows that identical pattern. From the beginning, ever since we have known a Bible, every Bible has been just like that, with every jot and every tittle in the same place. Every letter is counted and at the end of every book a summation is made so that the copyist, through the thousands of years before there was such a thing as a printing press, would be sure that his work was correct. This Hebrew Bible is the same Bible, jot for jot, tittle for tittle, page by page, dot by dot, that Jesus held in His hands.

Some six years ago there was discovered in a cave not far from the Dead Sea, in a place called Qumran, some manuscripts in an old jar. These priceless manuscripts included a complete copy of Isaiah and of Habakkuk. Since then many more manuscripts and fragments have been discovered, about 100 of them Biblical manuscripts. These manuscripts antedate by at least one thousand years the present Hebrew Old Testament manuscripts which we have. Yet as we look at those ancient manuscripts, one thousand years older than any that we have today, we discover that they are practically the same as the Masoretic text that is used in the publication of this Hebrew Bible. God's inerrant Word, through the years our final authority, is what God has written in heaven and the copy of that Holy Word is here in my hand.

Through the centuries human beings have tried to add to God's Holy Word. At the Council of Trent, in 1545, the Roman Catholic Church voted to include in God's Book all the volumes of the Apocrypha. But God decreed that they would not be part of His Book. And they are not in the Protestant Bible, the Bible that is the world's best seller. There is not a fair-minded Jew or a fair-minded Christian on earth today who would include in God's Holy Book the monstrous absurdities that you read in the Apocrypha. There were thirty-nine books in the Old Testament two thousand years ago and there are thirty-nine today.

There were men who wanted to add to the twenty-seven books of the New Testament. So they wrote epistles and they wrote gospels and they wrote apocalypses. But none of them were ever added to the twenty-seven books of the New Testament — they rotted away just like fruit tied on a tree. What did the Psalmist say? "For ever, O Lord, thy word *natsab,* thy word is fixed, thy word is settled in heaven." And the Bible that I hold in my hand is a copy of the original that God has inspired and kept inviolate in glory.

THE INCORRUPTIBLE WORD

The second word is a Greek word, found in the first chapter of I Peter, verses 23 through 25:

> Being born again [being saved], not of corruptible seed, but of incorruptible, by the word of God, which liveth and abideth for ever. For all flesh is as grass, and all the glory of man as the flower of grass. The grass withereth, and the flower thereof falleth away: But the word of the Lord endureth for ever. And this is the word which by the gospel is preached unto you.

The apostle does an unusual thing here. He takes a verse out of the fortieth chapter of Isaiah (verse eight): "The grass withereth, the flower fadeth: but the word of our God shall stand for ever." But he describes the Word of God with a Greek word: "We are born again, not of *phtharté,* corruptible or perishable seed, but of *aphtharté,* of incorruptible seed, by the word of God, which liveth and abideth for ever." So the apostle here is inspired to say that the Word of God not only endures forever, stands forever, abides forever, but it abides *aphthartos,* it abides incorruptible, it abides inerrant, it abides without mistake and without error.

Through all of the centuries and through all of the milleniums, God's sovereign grace cared for and protected His Holy Word so that it would come to us as a copy of that original in heaven. The Lord God, the Holy Spirit of the Lord who watched over the Incarnate Word in Bethlehem when Herod sought to destroy Jesus with the sword, watches over His written Word through the vicissitudes of the centuries. The same Lord God in heaven, the same Holy Spirit from above who preserved from corruption the Incarnate Word, who raised Jesus from the dead, is the same Holy Spirit of God, Sovereign, Almighty, who preserves from corruption this Word that I hold in my hand. The sovereign grace of God in His elective purpose that shall deliver us to heaven, that assures the salvation of His saints, is the same sovereign grace that keeps and preserves His Word today. The Holy Spirit of God that inspired it is the same Holy Spirit of God that keeps it. No council, no assembly, no convocation ever has been able to add to it or take away from it. "Born again . . . of incorruptible seed, by the word of God, which liveth and abideth for ever." To me that is one of the most miraculous things in all the earth.

It was not until about one thousand five hundred years after Jesus that printing was invented. During all of those centuries the Word had to be copied by hand. How was it preserved inerrant? How was it kept just like that original up in heaven? It is a very simple thing. God did it by the multiplicity of the manuscripts. So, if a scribe made an error in copying the Word of God, there would be thousands of other manuscripts with which to compare it, to detect any error. For God ordained that there should be thousands of manuscripts made of His infallible Word. And I say that that is a miracle.

One thousand five hundred years after Herodotus had written his history, there was only one copy of it in the whole world. One thousand two hundred years after Plato wrote his glorious classic, there was only one manuscript of it. To the present day, there is only one manuscript of the annals of Tacitus, there is only one manuscript of the Greek Anthology. We have just a few manuscripts today of Sophocles and Euripedes, of Thucydides, of Virgil and of Cicero. But there are thousands and thousands of copies of the Word of God, which can be compared to arrive at the original reading.

One of our Greek scholars has estimated that there are more than four thousand, one hundred five (4,105) ancient Greek manuscripts of the New Testament. Another one says that there are fifteen to thirty thousand ancient Latin versions of the Holy Scriptures. Another says that there are more than a thousand ancient versions (the translation of the Scriptures into other languages), besides the papyri that they are daily discovering in archaeological excavations, and besides the quotations you find in the Church Fathers. By comparing these thousands of manuscripts, it is easy to discover the original that God has inspired in heaven. If one copyist made an error, God prevented other copyists from making that error. Just as when one preacher departs from the faith, God raises up another preacher to be true to the message. If one church departs from the Book, God keeps another church true to the Gospel. If a whole denomination departs from the faith, God plans for another denomination to preach the Gospel of the grace of the Son of God. We are born again, we are saved, by incorruptible seed [*aphtharté*], "by the word of God, which liveth and abideth for ever" — kept inerrant by the sovereign grace of God.

PAGAN AND ECCLESIASTICAL PERSECUTIONS

My third word in this message is a Hebrew word found in Isaiah 40:6-8 (which Peter quoted in his first epistle in the verse we have just looked at):

> The voice said, Cry. And he said, What shall I cry? All flesh is grass, and all the goodliness thereof is as the flower of the

> field: The grass withereth, the flower fadeth: because the spirit of the Lord bloweth upon it: surely the people is grass. The grass withereth, the flower fadeth: but the word of our God shall stand *[yaqum]* for ever.

What does *yaqum* mean? It is translated here *shall stand.* *Yaqum* means *to rise,* with the imagery of something prostrate, crushed, ground under the heels, but made to stand up again. The import of the prophet's word is that in contrast to the short-lived things of earth, the Word of God though crushed, persecuted, despised, or attacked with intent to destroy, shall rise, shall stand, shall abide forever.

Against the Holy Bible, some of the most cruel and merciless of all of the persecuting powers of men have been dedicated. I am going to speak of three of them. First, *pagan persecution.* And out of the many successions of pagan persecution against those who held sacred this Bible, and the attempt to exterminate this Book, I choose one — the Diocletian persecution. Diocletian instituted the most violent and merciless assault against the Bible and the people of the Bible that the world has ever known.

In A.D. 303 Diocletian, Emperor of the Roman Empire, decreed that every Bible in the world should be destroyed and the people who possessed Bibles should be slain. So effective was that horrible, cruel onslaught that in about a year or two the persecutors supposed that they had eradicated the Bible from the face of the earth. Myriads of Christians laid down their lives when they were discovered loving the Word of God. Diocletian was told that Christians were a people of the Book, and that if the Book were destroyed the faith would cease to exist. So he sought to destroy the Book. Diocletian considered his drive of extermination so successful that over a burned and extinguished Bible he built a column and on it wrote these triumphant Latin words: *Extincto nomene Christianorum*: the name of Christian is extinguished. Christians were drowned in blood, consumed by fire — anguish, martyrdom, death!

But who succeeded the cruel Diocletian? The Emperor Constantine. He declared himself to be a Christian, though he was the Caesar of the Roman Empire. He took off the pagan symbols from the standards of his Roman army and the shields of his marching soldiers, and he placed on them the symbol of the cross of Jesus Christ. That marvelous transformation happened in A.D. 312. How many years was that after Diocletian had erected his column over a burned and destroyed Bible, saying that the very name of the Christians was extinct? Less than ten! "The grass withereth, the flower fadeth: but the word of our God shall stand [*yaqum,* abide] for ever."

Now I speak of a second persecution, an ecclesiastical persecution. Isn't it an almost inexplicable thing that the bitterest enemy of the Word of God should be the ecclesiastic churchman with a desire to destroy the Bible? Martin Luther was a churchman all his life, but he was a grown man when he said, "I have never seen a Bible."

When John Wycliffe sought to present this Holy Book in the vernacular, in the language of the people of England, he was marked out for death. The terrible Inquisition could not reach him before he had died, but the inquisitors dug up his body and burned it. When anyone was found with a copy of the Scriptures translated by John Wycliffe into English, the copy of the Bible was tied around his neck and he was openly burned at the stake. Because John Wycliffe had translated the Bible into English and had given it to the people, his dead body was burned and his ashes were strewn over the River Swift; but the River Swift runs into the Avon, the Avon runs into the Severn, the Severn runs into the sea, and the sea bathes the shores of the seven continents of the world. Wherever the waters of the sea carried the ashes of John Wycliffe, there also was borne the Word of God. "The grass withereth, the flower fadeth: but the word of God shall stand [*yaqum,* rise, endure] for ever."

THE ONSLAUGHT OF MODERN RATIONALISM

Now the last attack upon the Bible, an attack that continues during our lifetime, is the deadliest and the bitterest of all. It is the onslaught of modern rationalism. The leaders are the Wellhausens and the Bauers and the Strausses and the Tubingen Schools, who flourish over the face of the earth and who, in the name of scholarship and research, scoff and laugh at this Holy Book. They deny the Deity of Christ. They make fun of the supernatural. They scoff at the miracles of the Lord. They say that this Book is nothing other than a collection of the folklore, the tales, the myths, and the legends of an ancient people, and that one can read the same things among the Greeks, the Persians, the Hindus and the ancient Egyptians. They avow that the Bible is no more inspired than the Book of the Dead of the Egyptians or the Bhagavad Gita of the Hindus.

So deadly and so merciless has been the poison of rationalism in the schools, in the universities, in the seminaries, in the pulpits, until it has seemed that the prophecy of Voltaire, the infidel who died in 1788, would come to pass. Voltaire said, "One hundred years from my day there will not be a Bible in the earth except one that is looked upon by an antiquarian curiosity-seeker." And it has sometimes looked as though there might come to pass what Hume, the infidel, envisioned: "I see the twilight of Christianity," he said. Yet one hundred years from the time of Voltaire's prediction, a first edition of Voltaire's work sold in the market in Paris for eleven cents. And on that identical day, the British Government paid to the Czar of Russia $500,000 for the Codex Sinaiticus, a copy of the Word of God discovered by Tischendorf in the monastery on Mount Sinai! When Hume said, "I see the twilight of Christianity," he was much confused. He could not tell sunrise from sunset.

Last eve I paused beside the blacksmith's door
And heard the anvil ring the vesper chimes;
Then looking in, I saw upon the floor
Old hammers worn out with beating years of time.

"How many anvils have you had," said I,
"To wear and batter all these hammers so?"
"Just one," said he and then with twinkling eye,
"The anvil wears the hammers out, you know."

And so I thought, the anvil of God's Word
For ages skeptics' blows have beat upon,
Yet, though the noise of falling blows was heard,
The anvil is unharmed, the hammers are gone.

— JOHN CLIFFORD

It is sunrise and not sunset.

How many of us read books that are a thousand years old? Some of you may read Virgil, some of you may read Cicero, some of you may read Caesar. But you are doing it probably because it is required in the school that you attend. Who reads a book a thousand years old? Who even reads a book of religion? Did you ever see anybody sitting down and reading *The Avesta of the Parsees?* Reading *The Tripitaka* (The Three Baskets) of the Buddhists? Reading *The Veda Hymns* of the Hindus? Did you ever see anybody sitting down reading the six classics of Confucius? Who reads a book of religion? Who reads a book translated out of another language?

It is a rule of thumb that no book written in one language and translated into another has much opportunity of being circulated. For instance, a book written by a Spaniard has no opportunity for wide circulation outside of Spanish speaking nations. Who are the great authors in Turkey? Who are the authors in Brazil? Who are the authors in Afghanistan or China? We probably do not know whether those countries have any authors or not. Any book written in another language has no opportunity of circulation in another.

How long ago was the Bible written? Centuries and centuries. In what language was the Bible written? In Hebrew and Greek. Both Greek and Hebrew have been dead languages, as they call them, for thousands of years. And yet the Bible, translated from Hebrew and Greek into various tongues, is increasingly circulated among the tribes and nations of all the earth.

Diocletian broke not one of the strings on this glorious harp. The rationalists have not drowned in infidelity one word from this immutable revelation. The Bolingbrokes and the Humes and the Paines and the Voltaires have not shortened its life by one hour.

> The earth shall pass away, someday,
> But my Word shall not pass away.
> The sun may fade, the moon decay,
> But God's Word lives forever.
>
> The flags of nations may be furled,
> The mountains to the seas be hurled,
> One thing will still outlast the world,
> God's Word shall live forever!

"The grass withereth, the flower fadeth: but the word of our God [*yaqum*] shall rise, shall stand, shall endure for ever."

Build your faith, build your life, build your soul, build your hopes, build your destiny on the immutable, unchanging, inerrant Word of God. To receive God's testimony is to receive God Himself. To love God's Book is to love God Himself. To receive the Holy Word is to receive the Lord Himself. For God's Word is like God Himself — the same yesterday, today, and forever.

Chapter 10

The Preservation of the Word of God
(SECOND SERMON)

> Heaven and earth shall pass away, but my words shall not pass away (Matthew 24:35).

Is the Bible we hold in our hands the Word of God as God delivered it through the prophets and the apostles? How can we know? How can we be sure? Hundreds of years before the invention of the modern printing press the holy books were copied by hand. Did the scribes mutilate the text? Did they add to it and take away from it?

The assured results of scholarly inquiry say that the ending of Mark is lost, that the gospel of Mark stops in the middle of the story of the resurrection at verse 8 in chapter 16. They also say that the story of an angel coming down at stated intervals to stir up the water at the pool of Bethesda, recorded in John 5:4, is certainly spurious; that a copyist wrote the explanation on the margin of the book he was copying and the next scribe placed the note in the text itself. The passage about the Trinity in I John 5:7 is also an interpolation, they say.

If these passages are glosses, what about other passages? If some are false, how shall I be able to pick out the true? I must have an answer to these questions or else I have no foundation upon which to build faith in the revealed Word of God. I must *know* that the Word is God's Word and not man's interpolation.

We have a sure and certain answer. The same Lord God who inspired the holy prophets and apostles to write the Word also was careful through infinite and multiplied ways to preserve the true Word. That we possess the true text is demonstrable fact.

TEXTUAL CRITICISM

The scientific study of the preservation of the true text of the Holy Scriptures is called textual criticism. It is one of the most blessed and rewarding fields of inquiry in the theological world. Nothing could be more interesting or more pertinent to the student of the Bible.

One of the early presidents of the Southern Baptist Theological Seminary in Louisville, Kentucky, and one of the great Greek scholars of all time, was Dr. John A. Broadus. The son-in-law of Dr. Broadus, Dr. A. T. Robertson, himself a world famous Greek scholar, said that Broadus loved textual criticism. He said that in Broadus' last illness, in his fever and delirium, he would dictate long passages of New Testament criticism; and each word that he spoke and each observation that he made was wonderfully correct, even though he was delirious and speaking out of his mind.

The first New Testament in Greek was published by Erasmus in 1516, and for two hundred years his edition, the Textus Receptus, was supreme in the world. In the year 1611 the English King James Version was made from that text. It is not a bad text; it is substantially correct; but it was based on later manuscripts and left much to be wanted. Among the scholars of the theological world there arose an intense desire to find those manuscripts that went back many hundreds of years to the very beginning of the Christian era. Surely, somewhere, the Bible texts used by the early Fathers were preserved and in existence. Where were they? Thus began the long and patient search for the ancient manuscripts of the Scriptures. Its story is one of the most romantic among the chapters of textual criticism.

At first each New Testament book was a roll in itself and was circulated separately in the place to which it was inscribed and for whom it was written. For example, there are some scholars who think that Matthew was written for the Palestinian and Syrian Christians and was circulated especially by the Christians at Antioch. They say that Mark was written for the Christians at Rome and was circulated by the church at Rome. They say that Luke was written for the churches of Greece and was circulated by the churches of Macedonia. They say that John was written in Ephesus and was circulated especially in Asia. And thus it was that as years passed and the churches began to exchange gospels and epistles, our New Testament was finally gathered together.

THE CODEX

The change from a book roll to a codex, that is a leaf book, was brought to pass about A.D. 300. The Christians needed to find a passage quickly. Consequently the roll was cut up and the leaves were put together at the back so that they could be easily turned one after another. It was only after the codex supplanted the roll that we began to have a complete New Testament.

The codex was written in large, even, capital letters called uncials. With the beginning of the seventh century another kind of Greek manuscript begins to appear. It is called the minuscule, or cursive — a running hand written in much smaller letters. By the ninth century there were no more uncials. In our search for ancient manuscripts, therefore, we are seeking the codex written in large, capital letters.

Into this search great Greek scholars through the last several hundred years have poured their very lives. They have paid untold prices in toil and suffering in order to learn the true and original Word of God. Some of them have been like Tregelles, a scholar who lived in poverty, whom England allowed almost to starve to death, and who went blind deciphering the ancient documents. Other scholars have been like Tischendorf, who was sponsored by the German and Russian governments. He was a professor at Leipzig University and regarded himself as an instrument in the hands of God for the discovery and publication of ancient manuscripts of the New Testament.

God has signally blessed these and many other scholars in their search for the ancient writings. Possibly one of the most romantic and interesting stories of all time is the discovery of *Aleph*, the alphabetical designation for Codex Sinaiticus which was discovered by Tischendorf in a monastery at the base of Mt. Sinai in the deserts beyond the Red Sea. For centuries this prized Greek manuscript lay beneath the books and rubbish of the old monastery and was accidentally brought to light by Tischendorf.

Tischendorf had been traveling throughout the East and searching all the old libraries for texts of the Scriptures. In 1844 he came to the monastery of St. Catherine located at the foot of Mt. Sinai. In the hall of the covenant was a basket full of parchments used for starting fires. He was told that two similar basketfuls had already been used for burning. Tischendorf looked at the parchment leaves and recognized them immediately. They came from a copy of the Old Testament Greek Septuagint (a translation of the Hebrew into Greek), and they appeared to be from the most ancient manuscript he had ever seen. Being unable to conceal his joy, he aroused the suspicions of the monks and, though the lot was destined for the fire, the monks refused to let him have the codex, thinking it might have value of which they had been unaware. They finally gave him forty-three sheets of the codex but refused to give him more.

In the year 1859, this time sponsored by the Russian government (and therefore having an easier entrance into the Greek Orthodox Monastery of St. Catherine), Tischendorf came back with a commission from the Russian Emperor to secure the rest of the leaves. His second visit promised to be a complete failure. The codex had simply disappeared. In despair and disappointment the faithful scholar was again turning away empty-handed.

On the evening before he had arranged to depart he was

walking on the grounds with the steward of the monastery, a gracious person who asked him into his cell to share some refreshments. As they conversed the monk produced a bundle wrapped in red cloth. To Tischendorf's unutterable and indescribable delight, he found in the bundle not only the leaves he had seen before in the wastebasket but other parts of the Old Testament and the complete New Testament, the only such ancient Greek manuscript containing all the New Testament that had ever been found. Tischendorf said that when the monk placed that precious volume in his hands, he knew that he held in his hand "the most precious Biblical treasure in existence." It was made in about A.D. 350 about the time the codex was developed.

Tischendorf brought the manuscript to the Imperial Library at St. Petersburg and gave it the name of Aleph, the first letter in the Hebrew alphabet. On December 24, 1933, Aleph was purchased by the British government from Russia for five hundred thousand dollars and was placed in the British Museum. Upon my visit to London it was my great and inexpressible joy to look upon the pages of this sacred manuscript. I was reminded as I looked at it that on the same day that the British government paid one-half million dollars for this copy of the Bible, one of my friends bought a first edition of Voltaire for eleven cents.

But by no means is Aleph the only ancient codex that has been discovered. Codex A, Alexandrinus, is almost as old. It was also my joy to look upon its pages in the British museum. It is called Alexandrinus because it once formed a part of the library at Alexandria. It was presented to Charles I in 1628, by Cyril, the patriarch of Constantinople.

Another and equally ancient Greek manuscript is Codex B, also called Codex Vaticanus because it is in the Vatican Library at Rome. It was written about the same time as Aleph.

Still another and most interesting manuscript is Codex C, named also Codex Ephraem. It was brought from the East to Florence, Italy, in the sixteenth century and a few years later was deposited in Paris where it has remained ever since. This Codex is a palimpsest, which means that the parchment was used twice. Under the top, cursive Greek script, someone noticed that there were traces of writing in the uncial style. In the olden days, to save parchment which was most costly, some of the scribes just scraped off the top writing and used the parchment again. About the twelfth century someone worked this process on Codex C. They took the parchment, scraped and rubbed it to clean off the old writing in order to make it fit for use again. When this was done the skins were used to write down the discourses of Ephraem, a Syrian Father of the fourth century. What he had to say was not one one-thousandth part as valuable as the ancient writing, because the first writing was that of the New Testament. Since impressions of the old, uncial script, however, still were to be seen, the parchment was sacredly and earnestly kept. About seventy-five years ago chemicals were discovered which, when applied to the old manuscripts would revive their ancient form. It was thus that fragments of each book of the New Testament were brought to light in the palimpsest Codex C.

THE FATHERS

In our search for the verification of the true, exact Word of God, we not only have these ancient Greek codices, but we also have the many, many quotations from the sacred Scriptures by the Fathers of the Early Church.

Years ago a group of scholarly men met around a dinner table in England. During the conversation someone in the party asked a question no one present was able to answer. It was this: Suppose the New Testament had been destroyed and every copy lost at the end of the third century; could it be collected together again from the writings of the Fathers of the second and third centuries? Two months afterward, one of the company called upon Sir David Dalrymple, who also had been present at the dinner. Pointing to a table covered with books, Sir David said: "Look at these books. Do you remember the question about the New Testament and the Fathers of the Church? As I possessed all the existing works of the Fathers of the second and third centuries, I commenced to search, and I have found the entire New Testament except eleven verses."

The early Fathers of the Church, such as Polycarp of Smyrna, Papias of Hierapolis, Clement of Rome, Irenaeus of Lyons, Tertullian of Carthage, Clement of Alexandria, Origen and Eusebius of Caesarea, were marvelous expositors of the written Word. They quote long and extensively and accurately from all the books of the Bible. Through their eyes we look upon the pages of the Scriptures as they were in their original form and text.

Likewise, the many ancient versions of the holy books translated into other tongues bear witness to the exact word of the original text. There are thousands of ancient manuscripts of the Bible in the Latin, Syrian, Coptic and other languages. Every one of them helps to verify the true and exact Word of God.

THE PAPYRI

No more startling evidence of the true text of the Scriptures has even been found than that unearthed by the spade of the archaeologist. The ancient cities of Egypt, with their grand palaces and dismal rubbish heaps, were buried and hermetically sealed by the drifting sands of the desert. Digging beneath the sands, into the graves and cemeteries and ash heaps and streets of long-perished civilizations, the scholars unearthed contemporary records of the daily life of the people. Among other things they found that the people wrote of their affairs on thin, flimsy sheets called papyri, made from the stalk of the papyrus plant which grows profusely along the banks of the Nile. Elsewhere in the world these papyri sheets decayed and were destroyed, but in Egypt, under the sands, protected from the ravages of the elements, they were perfectly preserved.

Reading these bits and fragments from the pens of those

ancient peoples, the scholars made an astounding discovery. It was once thought that the language of the Greek New Testament was a special, holy, different kind of language, used just in the Bible, not to be found in any other literature of the world. The papyri changed all that. To the joy and delight of the archaeologist it was discovered that the common, ordinary, everyday language of the people was the language of the Greek New Testament, now called *Koiné* Greek. The discovery served to explain many idioms of the Bible. But it did far more. As the scholars continued to unearth these ancient papyri manuscripts from the waste and rubbish heaps of the cities of Egypt, they found many parts of the sacred Scriptures and many verifications that the Greek words used in the gospels and the epistles were current in everyday life. The Bible became even more a living, pulsating book.

OUR ASSURANCE OF THE TRUE WORD OF THE TEXT

It is thus that from every part of the ancient world, from the tombs, from the rubbish heaps, from the libraries, from the writings of the Fathers, from the versions, there comes evidence piled on top of evidence for the authenticity of the text of the Word of God. The multiplication of these ancient manuscripts is unbelievable. They come from every part of the ancient world, and they cover every portion of the New Testament and of the whole Bible. For example, one scholar estimates that there are 4,105 ancient Greek manuscripts of the New Testament. It has also been variously estimated that there are as many as 15,000 to 30,000 Latin versions of the Holy Scriptures. Beside these, there are at least 1,000 other early versions of the Sacred Word. When all those thousands of documents are checked, compared, combined, grouped, studied, we have a certain and final answer regarding the text.

When we remember that there is but a single manuscript that preserves the annals of Tacitus; when we remember that there is but a single manuscript that preserves the

Greek Anthology; when we remember that the manuscripts of Sophocles, of Thucydides, of Euripides, of Virgil, of Cicero are most rare and the very few in existence are, for the most part, very late; then we can see with what profusion of evidence God supported the truth of the transcription of His Sacred Word.

With complete and perfect assurance I can pick up my Bible and know that I read the revealed Word of God. The God who inspired it also took faithful care that it be exactly preserved through the fire and the blood of the centuries. When Jesus went away He said to His disciples: "These things have I spoken unto you, being yet present with you. But the Comforter, which is the Holy Ghost, whom the Father will send in my name, he shall teach you all things, and bring all things to your remembrance, whatsoever I have said unto you" (John 14:25, 26). The same blessed Paraclete, the Holy Spirit of God, who brought to the remembrance of the disciples the spoken word of Jesus that it might become indelible in the written word, also preserved the sacred writing from mutilation and destruction.

John sealed the last page of the sacred Scriptures with these awesome sentences:

> For I testify unto every man that heareth the word of the prophecy of this book, If any man shall add unto these things, God shall add unto him the plagues that are written in this book: and if any man shall take away from the words of the book of this prophecy, God shall take away his part out of the book of life, and out of the holy city, and from the things which are written in this book (Revelation 22:18, 19).

The Ancient of Days, through the centuries since, has kept the holy books as they were written. Where there have been the slightest additions or deletions or changes we know it and can easily separate the glosses from the true and inspired text. Each line, each letter, each syllable, has been kept for us even as the holy men of God spoke and wrote, "moved by the Holy Spirit" (II Peter 1:21).

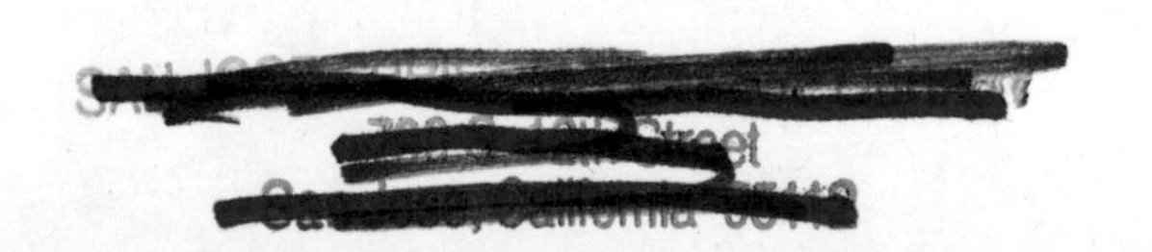